Barbizon Days

J. F. Millet

Jean Francois Millet

Jean Francois Millet

BARBIZON DAYS

MILLET—COROT—ROUSSEAU—BARYE

By CHARLES SPRAGUE SMITH

NEW YORK
A. WESSELS COMPANY
1903

PRESS OF
BRAUNWORTH & CO.
BOOKBINDERS AND PRINTERS
BROOKLYN, N. Y.

To
HILDA

INTRODUCTION

A decade of years ago, we pitched our summer tent at Bourron, a little hamlet on the borders of the Forest of Fontainebleau; or rather we occupied another's tent, for our dwelling was a grey stone cottage similar to that of the peasants—our neighbors and friends. The Forest itself was only a few rods distant and my study, the summer through, was in the open air and under the boughs of one of its noble trees.

Sitting at my neighbors' board, when their day's work was done, roaming the wood in all directions, searching out especially the haunts of the artists, the months glided away all too fast. There were not hours enough in which to write of all the artists I would have selected as themes.

These sketches are not art criticism, they are but the chronicle of that summer. If they make clearer the relation between nature and art, suggest that art's alphabet is everywhere awaiting only the seeing eye, or if I have been able to give again in part the inspiration obtained from that summer's converse with the strong, this record of Barbizon Days will have accomplished its purpose.

CHARLES SPRAGUE SMITH

New York, July 1, 1902

Group of Jules Dupré

Group of Jules Dupré

The Forest of Fontainebleau

The Forest of Fontainebleau

IF we call up before our minds the places made notable by great achievements in modern art history, Paris and other centres of European life suggest themselves. The only exception to this rule, so far as I know, is a tiny hamlet, a single street, bounded on the one side by the Forest of Fontainebleau and on the other by a broad plain. It is asserted that, between 1825 and 1860, there gathered about an inn table in this hamlet the largest group of men of creative power with the brush, that have ever assembled anywhere since the Renaissance.

A day in the Forest and in the hamlet of Barbizon now, after a half century's interval, cannot give the same impressions of either wood or village which those "men of 1830" received. For the forest has been transformed, its solitudes have been made accessible, and thus, to the artist, profaned; and the hamlet has been bound to the great world, not merely by broad carriage roads, displacing a foot-path across the forest, but even by a railroad that passes Rousseau's and Barye's cottages and Millet's atelier.

Yet, if one follows day after day the lure of the wood-paths and loiters or hastens as the hour and Nature invite, the forest, persuaded that you are not a trifler, will admit you to so intimate a companionship that you can think away every profanation; and, to recall the hamlet seek out the less frequented villages, even though remoter from the wood, and recreate, with features borrowed from one and the other, that old peasant street, hidden away from the world, leading from the plain of labor to the cow-gate, the opening into the wood, through which each morning the herdsman drove the cattle of the village to their pasture in the forest.

The Forest of Fontainebleau cannot have been in 1830 in any true sense a primeval forest. Man had used it too long for his own purposes. Some one of the early Capetian dukes or kings built in its centre a donjon, already old in the time of Louis VII. (12th century) when we have the first historical record of its existence. In later centuries, a Renaissance château, largely the work of François I., displacing the feudal donjon, became the favorite residence, outside of Paris, of the Kings of France. And in the forest glades, men and women, whom

The Sully

The Sully

history names, hunted and disported themselves. Numberless paths traversed the wood and a road had been built about it as early as in the time of Henri IV. (1589–1610).

The forest had not only lost, by 1830, in a large degree, its primeval savagery, its mystery of the unexplored; but it had never been vast enough for a true empire of Nature. It is only fifty miles in circumference, not more than ten in average breadth, and there are neither lakes nor mountains in its entire domain, only shallow pools and low ranges of hills.

In a primeval forest the sunlight scarce penetrates; the trees are too tall, their crests too serried to allow the sun's rays to glide between. There is no green undergrowth, for the soil is buried deep beneath the brown leaves. You cannot go far in a straight line. Bristling barriers or long, narrow mounds, the dying or dead boles of old forest kings, obstruct the path. Bird-notes are rare. Mountain tops reveal a world of pine and oak, of maple and birch, sweeping in grand undulations to the horizon's verge. Between the hills, blue lakes rest, free of all intrusion save the native life of the woods. In mid-air, above a lake, an eagle or an osprey floats.

The Forest of Fontainebleau, in the 19th century at least, knew nothing of all this. And, since its limited area with its many centuries of subjection to man forbade long ago that it should be a primeval forest, I hold they have done right who have admitted air and light to the wood, and, completing the work of earlier foresters, have made of the whole a grove, not of one character but manifold; now choked with undergrowth, now stretching in vast open templed aisles, and now, with lesser trees withdrawn a space paying homage to some grand oak that sheltered perhaps the first French king and survives the last.

The Master of it all, the Lord Creator of its surpassing beauty, is the Sun, who fills its atmosphere with life, bands its trunks, drips in diamonds from myriad leaf-tips at the sunset hour, makes gold-yellow the fresh green of the under-growth, bejewels heather and vagrant flowers and rests a mellow sheen on lichen-covered rocks and in open glades. The Forest of Fontainebleau has to-day a beauty all its own and every whit as overpowering, when you have come under its spell, as the grand, stern beauty of primeval Nature.

A "Mare"

I have said that the wood has no lakes, only shallow pools. A good friend and neighbor has told me once and again I must not leave the forest without paying at least one visit to the beautiful Mare aux Fées, the Fairies' Pond, and I have just returned therefrom. The way thither had a charm of noble woods, cleansed of decay and pruned of after-growth. The trees dwarfed as I drew nearer the Mare. I reached it at last, a tiny shallow pond, half choked with reeds and whatever else Nature sends forth from her storehouse to do battle with water and make of ponds first marshes and then rich meadow land.

But if the wood is without the charm of lakes, it has an element of power and variety that few primeval forests can boast. Eight to ten ranges of low sandstone hills traverse it from east to west, separated often only by narrow gorges. Broken tables of stone are heaped up in fantastic piles in the gorges' bottom or tilted against each other on the slopes. Huge blocks are strewn broadcast everywhere among the trees. The gorges of Apremont and Franchard suggest Milton's description of the battle between the hosts of heaven and hell, where hills were plucked up by their roots and hurled, encountering mid-air, the wrack falling to earth. To the forest this rock scenery adds a note of savagery, and Fenimore Cooper must have had this feature especially in mind when he said that the Forest of Fontaine-bleau exceeded in savage variety anything he had ever seen in America.

Such then, though more primeval in places and more reserved to the few, was the forest which the men of 1830 knew.

The Fontainebleau villages have a rich and varied charm of novelty and art-sugges-tion for the eye accustomed only to the countryside of the New World. But the masters of 1830 had not such other-world images in their eyes. The Norman peasant, Millet had seen elsewhere in France villages differing only in unimportant details. The distinctive feature of Barbizon, to the men of 1830, was that its isolation served as a screen to shut away all suggestions of mani-fold activities and interests, and concentrate attention upon man in his few primeval re-lations to Nature—man as husbandman, man as husband and father.

To-day, apart from its associations with Millet and his friends and its setting of plain

The Chaos of the Gorges of Apremont

The Chaos of the Gorges of Apremont

and forest, Barbizon yields in rural charm and artistic suggestion to other Fontainebleau villages.

Montigny looks down from its towered church, overtopping huddled gray cottages, upon the Loing as it glides, a modest river, between banks sentineled with closely trimmed poplar trees. By the riverside, near the tiny bridge, where the white and color of kerchief and apron can catch the sunlight, the women of the hamlet wash their clothes. If you linger till the noon hour, the exhaling river breath will fuse the green of the poplar leaves into a silver haze.

Through Moret and past Grez the Loing flows also; Moret has noble turreted gateways and Grez a church more picturesque than that of Montigny, riverscapes more alluring, and a ruined château said to be of Queen Blanche, mother of St. Louis.

Thomery has covered the high walls of its narrow streets, the street ends and façades of its houses with lush vine leaves; and the heavy green pendant bunches are the chasselas, best of all the grapes of Northern France. Larchant, a tiny village away from the forest, was to Millet and his friends a shrine of yearly pilgrimage. It was once a

walled town of some importance with a noble
church, contemporary of Notre Dame of
Paris, and sacred to Mathurin, a local saint,
born here in the fourth century, whose
miracle-working tomb it covered. But the
Calvinists sacked the church in 1567, and
two centuries later, 1778, a conflagration
swept the town and completed the work
of the iconoclasts. A solitary dismantled
tower rises high above the plain; around
and over it multitudes of black-winged
birds hover, as in Millet's painting of the
Gréville church.

In the old days of post travel, Chailly
was the last relay station on the high road
from Paris to Fontainebleau. Barbizon, a
hamlet of Chailly, across the fields and about
a mile away, was formed of a single short
street a half-mile in length joining plain
and forest. The houses or farmsteads lining
it consisted of open courts, where the manure
was thrown, the cows milked, the poultry
fed, the children played. About each court
stood the stables and the dwelling. There
was no church, no market-place, no inn,
not even a graveyard in the hamlet. The
only access to it was afforded by the almost
impassable road across the fields from Chailly

The Loing at Montigny

and a path through the forest, that left the highway between Chailly and Fontaine-bleau.

Barbizon was discovered, Will Low tells us, in 1824. Two artists, Claude Aligny and Philippe Le Dieu, had come to Fontaine-bleau to visit their friend Jacob Petit, direc-tor of a porcelain manufactory. The three started one day to explore the forest in quest of themes for the brush. By nightfall they had lost their way. Following the sound of a horn and of tinkling bells they came upon a cow-herd, who told them they were in the gorge of Apremont and six miles from Fontainebleau. He led them to the nearby village of Barbizon and the house of François Ganne, a thrifty peasant, who with his young wife occupied two rooms, one as sleeping apartment, the other for his trade as tailor and for the sale of wine. Ganne could provide food but not lodging, so the cow-herd let them pass the night on the straw with his cattle. The next morning they explored the portion of the wood near-est the hamlet, the Bas Bréau, I presume, and were so amazed and delighted there-with that Aligny and Le Dieu insisted that Ganne should receive them as permanent lodgers. Ganne saw his advantage and consented, ceding to them his bedroom and, with his wife, taking up his own abode in the barn.

Word was brought back to Paris of the discovery of this bit of unspoiled primitive Nature only a day's walk distant from that most modern of European capitals, and the next year the artists invaded the place, occupying every available nook and corner. Ganne provided food for all. Those who could not find lodgings in Barbizon stopped in Chailly at the White Horse, among others Corot, Rousseau, Barye, Diaz.

In 1830 Ganne bought a large barn and fitted it up as a two-story hotel with windows on the north side for studios. On the ground floor there was an immense dining-room and café with billiard table and balls as large as a man's fist. All the artists took lodgings with him. In the height of the season some slept on the top of the table and others in the barn loft on the straw. Between 1825 and 1860 nearly every French artist and representative artists from every other civilized nation visited Barbizon.

It was a glad and sane "vie de Bohème" these men led, to judge from Low's report.

Larchant

Each season one was chosen as leader and the joint pleasures took on a more serious or boisterous tone according to the leader's temperament. Under Gérôme they decorated the panels of the dining-room; under Amédée Servint, the troupe invaded in masquerade on horseback the outlying villages.

It was the law of the place to rise early, the most diligent at five, and be off to the forest, the fun not commencing till after the dinner hour. Each newcomer had to smoke Diaz's pipe. If the color of the smoke were iridescent he was declared a colorist, if gray a classicist. The most jovial festival of all was at the marriage of Ganne's youngest daughter to Eugène Cuvelier, an artist of Arras. The feast was held in a barn, candles in tin baskets served as lanterns, ivy as decoration. Rousseau and Millet were the chief decorators. Corot led the bottle dance, first slowly, then fast and faster. Empty bottles were placed at equal distances from each other and the dancers had to pass between. Whoever tipped over a bottle was out of the dance. He who survived received the prize, a flower from the bride.

Corot, Rousseau and Barye came in 1830

and stayed after the others had left. Corot came only irregularly; Rousseau after 1849 spent only his summers there; Barye spent summer and fall until his death; to Millet it was home all the year round.

The good "vie de Bohème" has vanished with the artists from Barbizon never to return. But, though the hamlet itself has been transformed, its setting remains essentially unchanged.

The plain of labor stretches away, broken by clumps of trees, hamlets, towns, to Paris in the distance. In its fields men and women are sowing, reaping, gleaning, driving cattle, sheep to pasture, watching sheep by night; the old farm at the village end and the towering hayricks remain, and still, from the tower of Chailly church, the Angelus calls at the sunset hour.

Still in the Bas Bréau, noblest wilderness of all the forest and at the very door of Barbizon, the grand trees speak as they spoke to Rousseau; still in open glades the play of light and shadow lures and witches as it did Diaz; still the gorges of Franchard offer the background for scenes of animal life they gave to Barye. The cattle of Troyon are still at pasture in the meadows, and so

Millet and Rousseau

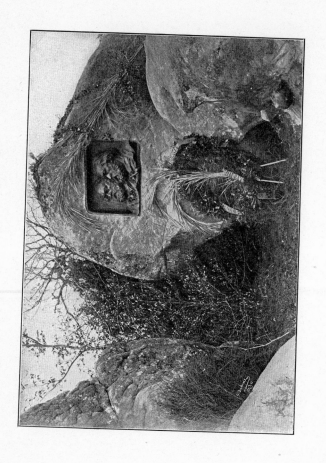

everywhere Nature offers, essentially unchanged, the originals whereof the canvases
of 1830 are the art interpretations. Corot
only is absent in spirit, for the sun-steeped
haze and the idyllic tone of his best canvases are not of Fontainebleau.

The artists who have supremely expressed the genius of the place, are the two
whose medallions have been set in the rock
near the old cow-gate, Millet and Rousseau;
Millet as interpreter of human life indoors
and out, and of those landscapes which
spring held up before him at his studio
door, when the air was moist yet clear and
the gnarled apple trees clothed themselves
for a moment with surpassing glory; Rousseau as interpreter of the woods. Forest-
ward the empire is all his. His single
steadfast purpose to be revealer of the trees
to man has made each noble stem, each
bosky group, his own.

Before 1830 Fontainebleau, plain and
forest, was as beautiful as to-day, grander
perhaps, but inarticulate; now it is voiceful
everywhere, and it will not soon lapse back
into silence.

We are too close to those men of Barbizon to determine whether or not they

created immortal works, and yet, one thing at least we may affirm without fear of erring: some of their canvases, as the "Sheep-Fold at Night" of Millet and the "Hoar Frost" of Rousseau, will long offer defiance to forgetfulness.*

* Both paintings are in Mr. Walter's gallery in Baltimore.

Entrance to Millet's Studio

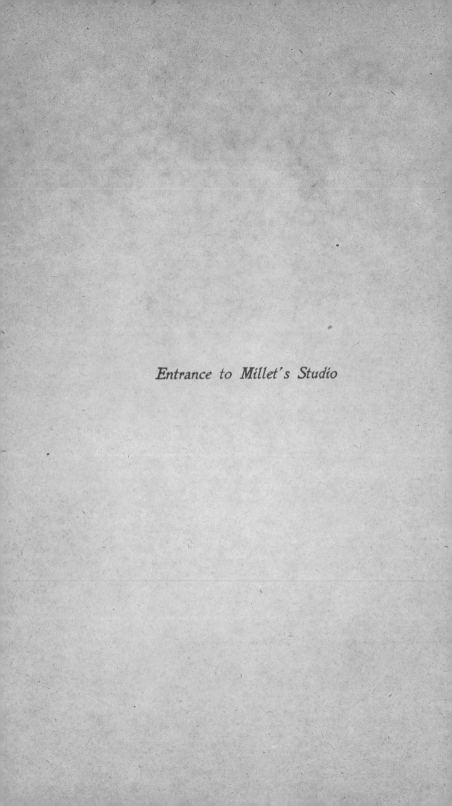

Entrance to Millet's Studio

Millet

Church which appears in
"The Angelus"

Millet

Those lives are worthiest that strike deepest root in the soil of our common life and are yet most responsive to the inspirations that come from the spaces beyond.

They are akin to the century-old children of the wood, that grasp tenaciously the black subsoil of the forest and aspire steadfastly toward the sunlight. Both grow gnarled and gray in the struggle, the tree and the man. The stancher, the longer-lived of the twain, speaks often courage to his feebler comrade. Where such comradeship has existed, the spirit of those long communings lingers in the still forest.

There is a life we would talk over with the trees of the Forest of Fontainebleau, one that, wearied with the work, the disappointment and the pains of life, came to them constantly for sympathy and drew as constantly renewal of strength from their comradeship.

Jean-François Millet found the work given him to do, and therein he implanted his life. Its fruits were rugged, harsh to the taste of his generation. He might have drawn, from shallower soil, that which pleased. But his simple, peasant nature, close in its qualities to the homely, industrious, fruit-bearing earth; akin in its tenacity of purpose to the firm-rooted oaks of his beloved forest, refused and refused again and turned back to work and suffer.

The canvases into which his experiences and aspirations; his life, were wrought, the children born of his constant pain and want, are freed now, and while he rests, as the forest trees rest, when their work is accomplished, these immortal ones are making the mystery of night more sensible, are deepening the religious sentiment in an age that needs that quickening, are intoning in grand, sober, rugged strophes the epic of toil.

Jean-François Millet was born the 4th of October, 1814, at Gruchy, and was the second of nine children. Henley says: "In the commune of Gréville, on the iron-bound coasts of la Manche, stands the little hamlet of Gruchy. It is built at the sea's edge, on the granite cliffs of la Hague, overlooking the stormy waters of Cherbourg Roads; but it is situate, for all that, in a fertile and pleasant valley, rich in grass,

Millet's Birthplace at Gruchy

(Elder sister standing in the doorway)

corn and wood, covered with herds and peopled with a race of husbandmen." The hamlet consisted of from twenty to twenty-five houses, and Millet said : "A stranger was rarely seen there, and such a silence reigned that the clucking of a hen or the cackling of a goose created a sensation." The village life was a patriarchal one. In the winter, the women sewed and spun, while the men wove baskets, and, as they worked, the old fables of the country were retold and the *noëls* sung.

The home of the Millets, Yriarte describes as "a long, low house of unhewn gray stone, roughly cemented together, capped with a high-pitched thatched roof. An old, gnarled vine half hides one part of the front under its green leaves." This type of peasant-house is a very common one to-day in Normandy and Brittany, though tiles have frequently displaced the thatch.

Although the means were straitened, an open-handed hospitality ruled. The wayfarer and the beggar were always welcomed to a full share of warmth and nourishment, as the ancient traditions of that part of France enjoin. The father was of a simple, gentle, devout nature. He was " passionately fond

of music and the precentor of the Gruchy
church, where he led and trained a choir
that was the envy and admiration of all the
countryside." He had a tender and reverent
love for Nature, and was ever pointing out
to his son the beauty of the landscape, as a
whole, or of the little and greater things
that composed it, the grass, the trees. The
neighbor's house, half-hidden behind a swell
of the field, impressed him as a picture.
The son recalls him moulding in clay and
carving in wood.

The mother was descended from the
Henry du Perron, a family of rich farmers,
regarded at one time as among the gentry of
the region. Simple, pious, devoted to her
family, and wholly submissive to her husband's will, she passed her life chiefly in the
fields and stables. For, it was, we are told,
the custom of the country that the wife
should perform the work of an out-of-door
laborer, while the headship within doors remained in the hands of the husband's mother.

The strong personalities of the Gruchy
home were the grandmother and the great-
uncle. The former, Louise Jumelin, widow
of Nicolas Millet, was a peasant woman of
the best type, industrious, clear-headed, born

to command. Her family was "old country stock, strong heads and warm hearts." She is described as "consumed by religious fire, severe for herself, gentle and charitable toward others, passing her life in good works, and with the ideal of sainthood constantly before her eyes."* She was so scrupulous and modest, touching her own conduct, that she invariably sought the counsel of the village curate, whenever a doubt arose about any action of her life. "Her religion blended itself," Millet said, "with a love of Nature. All that was beautiful, grand, terrible, appeared to her as the work of the Creator, whose will she respected and adored." François was her favorite grandson, her godson and the oldest boy, and she gave to him the name of her chosen saint, François d'Assise. Millet recalls her entering his bedroom one morning, when he was but a little lad. "Awake, my little François," she said; "if you only knew how long a time the birds have been singing the glory of the good God!"

The uncle, Charles Millet, was one of

* Henry Naegely says that Millet's portrait of his grandmother represented her with large eyes, a firm, rather wide mouth, curving with kindness, and a powerful face, refined and softened by a shadow of mysticism. Her attire was always rigid in neatness and simplicity.

those priests whom the revolution had unfrocked. He stanchly refused to swear allegiance to the constitution, believing that it infringed the rights of the Pope. During the Reign of Terror, he was proscribed and had many hairbreadth escapes. When again at liberty to assume his sacred office, he joined, with the work of priest and teacher, that of peasant. We see him, a giant in strength, carrying huge blocks of granite to build a wall, or holding the plough handle, with breviary in pocket and cassock tucked up to his waist, entering, in a word, into all the labors of peasant life with the energy and zest of a man of vigorous and helpful temperament; or— a gentler side of his nature—teaching the poor children of the commune.

François' early education was pushed quite far, it would seem, for a peasant's son. He began the study of Latin at twelve and, though compelled to devote a large part of his time—later his entire time—to the fields, he conquered early the elementary difficulties of the language and acquired a love therefor which continued all through life. Virgil and the Latin Bible were from this time forward favorite books.

MILLET

From the years of his maturity there comes a story which interlinks itself with these earliest days. Millet was enabled, for the first time in many years, through an order received for a painting, to revisit his childhood's home. The grandmother, whose pride and hope he had been, and the weary mother, had awaited long his coming, but death had already overtaken them.* Sad memories blended therefore with the joy of the return with his children to the old home. He wandered everywhere, sketching all the beloved, familiar things. One evening, as he was returning homeward, the Angelus sounded from the church tower of the little village of Éculleville. He entered. An old priest was kneeling at the altar. He approached him and waited until he rose from his knees. Then, touching him gently on the shoulder, he said, in a low voice; "François." It was the Abbé Jean Lebriseux, his former teacher. They embraced weeping. Then the old priest

---

* The grandmother died in 1851, the mother two years later, with Millet's name on her lips. Millet, on receiving the news, took out his Bible, and read the story of Tobit and his wife. The idea of "*l'Attente*" came to him at the thought of his mother's longing for him, and he made a sketch immediately. The painting was not exhibited till 1854. As his share of the inheritance, Millet asked for the great oak cupboard and his great-uncle's books, and begged that the ivy growing over the house be left untouched.

asked, "And the Bible, François, have you forgotten it, and the psalms, do you re-read them?" "They are my breviaries," Millet answered. "It is from them I draw forth all that I do." "You loved Virgil well in the old days." "I love him still."

The home library was composed almost wholly of religious works, brought there by the grandmother and uncle. Sensier mentions The Confessions of Saint Augustine; The Lives of the Saints; Saint François de Sales; Saint Jerome, especially his letters; the religious philosophers of Port-Royal; Bossuet; Fénelon; the Bible in Latin, and Virgil.

The peasants of Gruchy were farmers rather than fishermen; thus the lad knew all the phases of the peasant-farmer's life from personal experience. But he knew the ocean also. In one of his reminiscences to his biographer, Sensier, he described an event that befell on All-Saints'-Day. A terrible storm was raging, the villagers were gathered in the church. Suddenly a seaman appeared at the door, crying out that a number of ships were being swept ashore and upon the rocks. He called for volunteers; fifty men rose and accompanied him.

The peasants saw from the cliffs five ships,
in quick succession, broken upon the rocks
and all on board drowned. Many other
ships met a like fate on the following day.
The boats sent to the rescue were overturned
and the men could render no assistance.
One ship drove in between two rocks and
the crew escaped. François, noticing a
heap upon the shore covered with a sail
cloth, lifted a corner and saw a mountain of
corpses.

So the years passed until 1832. These
eighteen years form the first period of
Millet's life. To the influences that surrounded him during this germinating age,
as well as to his inherited traits, he owed
the fundamental elements of his character
and expression. The lad was intelligent,
studious, persistent. Had he not been, he
would not have mastered the Latin Bible
and Virgil. The artistic element, which
appeared as a germ in the grandmother and
labored awkwardly for expression in the
father, was already moving actively in him.
The engravings of the Bible excited a desire
of imitation. During the siesta, while the
rest slept, he made sketches of whatever was
before him, " the garden, the stables, the

fields with the sea for horizon, and often the animals that passed." The father only simulated sleep and watched with content the developing facility of the son; he had the longing without the power; perhaps the *bon Dieu* had given both to François.

He who was later to be the painter of peasant life had received from the *bon Dieu* exactly that early training necessary to fit him for his work. If one thing were lacking therein, if one thing is lacking in Millet's representations of peasant life, it is sunlight, glad resting, joy, laughter.

Yet joy, undimmed by care, can hardly have come oftentimes to that Gruchy household; the mouths were too many, the soil was too old, too obstinate, the temper of the ruling spirits too serious; the house itself, to judge from the photograph, is stern and bare. The mother, a gentlewoman, bearing nine children and doing the rude work of the field and stable, never complaining, yet always weary; the gentle, simple-hearted father; the strong-spirited, devout grandmother; the rising with the sun; the incessant toiling throughout the slow year; and, for reward, existence and the consciousness of duty done—everything here im-

MILLET

pressed upon the plastic mind of him who
was part of it all the serious meaning of
life, its worthiness and its rude grandeur too,
where the burden was borne with the man-
liness and womanliness he saw exhibited in
those nearest to him. No master could
ever instruct him as Nature had done; he
had the knowledge now; he did not yet
know, he would not learn for nearly a score
of years how to give it expression.

One day, on returning from mass, he
noticed a peasant, an old man with stooping
figure, and was astonished at the perspective.
It came to him as a kind of revelation.
Hastening home, he made a charcoal sketch.
His father, on seeing it, was profoundly
moved and said: "My poor François, I see
well that you torment yourself with this
idea. I would gladly have sent you to learn
this profession of painter, which they say is
so fine, but I could not. You are the oldest
of my boys, and I had too much need of
you; but now the others are growing up
and I will not hinder you from learning
what you so much desire to know. We
will presently go to Cherbourg and ascertain
if you have in truth the talent to gain your
living in this occupation."

[37]

The lad finished for the Cherbourg visit two sketches, the first, of two shepherds and a hill-slope with sheep. One shepherd was playing a flute and the other listening. The shepherds wore the jackets and wooden shoes of his country. The hillock with pasturing sheep was an apple orchard belonging to his father. The second drawing represented a starry night, with a man coming out of a house carrying bread which a second received. Sensier says that he has looked at this drawing for thirty years and it is the work of a man who already knows the great drift of art. One would believe it a sketch by a seventeenth century artist.

The painter, Mouchel, whom François Millet and his father consulted in Cherbourg, refused to believe these drawings the work of the lad. When finally convinced by their repeated protestations, he cried out to the father: "Eh bien, vous serez damné, pour l'avoir gardé si longtemps, car il y a chez votre enfant l'étoffe d'un grand peintre!"

The career of François Millet was decided; his father even urged him toward it.

The lad entered the studio of M. Bon Dumoucel, commonly called Mouchel. Sen-

sier describes this first master as an original
genius, self-educated, loving art and the
country. Although the journal of the
following years is somewhat vague in details,
the broad lines are sufficiently clear. Millet
remained only two months with Mouchel
and learned less from him than from his
work in the Cherbourg museum, studying
and copying from the old masters.* His
father's death, in 1835, recalled him to
Gruchy, and he remained there for a time,
the charge of affairs naturally devolving upon
him as the oldest son. But his work in
Cherbourg had excited a great deal of local
interest, and the notabilities bestirred themselves in order to prevent his going back to
the life of the farm. When his grandmother
heard thereof, she said: "My François, we
must accept the will of God; your father,
my Jean-Louis, said you should be a painter;
obey him and return to Cherbourg."

On his return he studied with another
painter, Langlois, a pupil of Gros, but the
relationship as before is represented as merely
a nominal one. He worked in the museum
and "read everything, from the *Almanach*

---

* The museum contained good paintings by Dutch and Flemish
masters.

Boiteux of Strasburg to Paul de Kock, from Homer to Béranger, and, with passion, Shakespeare, Walter Scott, Byron, Cooper, Goethe's Faust and the German ballads." Victor Hugo and Chateaubriand especially impressed him. His biographer adds a paragraph which shows how just was Millet's native art sense. "He would have wished to reject all of his (Hugo's) exaggerations, in order to compose for his own use a Victor Hugo of two or three volumes, which would have been the Homer of France."*

Langlois was so impressed with the power and originality of his pupil, that he addressed, in August, 1836, a most enthusiastic letter about him to the mayor and members of the municipal council, asking their assistance, in order to send him to Paris, and gave them his personal pledge that posterity would do them honor, if they consented thereto, "for having been the first, on this occasion, to assist in endowing the fatherland with one great man more." The municipal

---

*Theocritus and Burns were later great favorites. He said: "The reading of Theocritus proves to me more and more that one is never so much Greek as in reproducing very naïvely impressions, it matters little where received, and Burns also proves that to me." In 1864 he began the study of Italian, in order to read Dante in the original.

council voted him an annuity of four hundred francs, to which the general council for the Department of la Manche added later six hundred francs. This grant, Millet said, did not continue long and was far from meeting his expenses. *

Dismissed with the devout, patriarchal exhortations of his grandmother, Millet reached Paris in January, 1837. He says of himself at this period: "I came to Paris with my ideas all formed in art, and I have not judged it *a propos* to modify them. I have been more or less fond of such and such masters, or such and such form of expressing art; but I have made no changes in the fundamentals."

He was proud, sensitive, shy, awkward, and had, in consequence, many difficulties and unpleasant experiences in establishing himself in the capital. At first he made no attempt to enter upon a regular course of study. While wandering hither and thither he entered the Louvre, as it were by haphazard, and lived therein a month. Michelangelo impressed him most, thereafter

* 600 francs were voted unanimously by the Municipal Council the first year. The following year the annuity was reduced to 400 francs and was only secured by the mayor's casting-vote. In 1839 the annuity of Cherbourg was withdrawn.

the early masters, the great Italians of the Renaissance, Murillo in his portraits, Ribera, Poussin and Lesueur of the French school. "I loved," Millet said, "everything that was powerful, and I would have given all of Boucher for a single nude of Rubens." Rembrandt blinded him at first; he felt he could only approach him gradually. He never made but one copy of the masters, and that, in a single hour and without premeditation, of Giorgione's "Concert." In the Luxembourg, he saw only theatrical effects and cared for nothing save the work of Delacroix.

He said later : "After Michelangelo and Poussin, I have held to my first liking for the early masters, for those subjects simple as infancy, for those unconscious expressions, for those beings who say nothing but feel themselves overburdened with life, or who suffer patiently without cries, without complainings, who bear the oppression of human law and have not even the idea of calling anyone to account for it." Michelangelo and Poussin remained his life-favorites, and there is much in his work that suggests both, Poussin's strong, sober coloring and absence of sensuous qualities, and Michelangelo's ruggedness and strength of line.

He was homesick and utterly solitary, for he did not dare to speak to anyone from fear of being laughed at. Naturally he wished to return to the Gruchy home, but the Louvre held him.

He put off for a long time entering a studio, partly through native shyness, partly because he was not drawn toward the notable artists of the day. He chose at last the studio of Paul Delaroche, apparently as a kind of *pis aller*, but he was too original and unadaptable to fit into the life of the place. His comrades of the *atelier* dubbed him "*l'homme des bois.*" His figures surprised them, but they looked upon him as bizarre, revolutionary and without a future. He left the studio soon, but returned for a time at Delaroche's personal entreaty. The master recognized the strength of the pupil, but it apparently rather startled him than otherwise, for he had not the knowledge or skill requisite to guide it. In 1839, when Millet was preparing to compete for the *Prix de Rome*, Delaroche told him he should use his influence that year to secure the scholarship for another of his pupils; the following year he would support Millet's claims. Millet, indignant at what he considered the unfairness of this procedure, withdrew definitively from Delaroche's studio.

Thenceforth Millet was his own guide. He hired with a comrade from the Delaroche studio, Louis-Alexandre Marolle, a little attic studio, and worked also in the evenings from the living model and the antique. Millet was then, as always afterward, excessively shy and awkward. His friend, Marolle, served him as medium of communication with the rest of the world, accompanying him everywhere and acting as spokesman. A great amount of light work was thrown off at this period, in order to secure funds wherewith to exist, for example, pastels in imitation of Watteau and Boucher. The highest price received therefor was twenty francs, while portraits sold as low as five francs. But he was working diligently meantime, reading the best books he could find on the human form, and especially everything connected with Michelangelo, whom, Sensier says, "he never ceased to regard as the highest expression of art," and whom Millet himself describes as "that one who haunted me all my life."

We have followed Millet's course during

these earliest years, step by step, watching
the unfolding of his nature. It is already
plain that his talent is too original, his will
too restive under rules imposed by others, to
follow in the beaten path. If there is suffi-
cient native strength within him, backed
by persistency, and fortune is not too rigorous,
l'homme des bois will subject a field unto
himself, in untilled ground, and broaden the
domain of art. The ten years that follow
his leaving Delaroche's studio are the ones
in which this question is decided. His
nature slowly grows toward its maturity, his
consciousness of the work given him to do
becomes distinct, and his resolve to do this
and naught else so tempered by adversity
that it can hold steadfast.

He married twice during these years;
first, in 1841, a delicate girl, who only
lived two and a half years, and again, in
1845, the brave, strong woman who was
his courageous helpmeet until the end.*
The greater part of this period was spent in
Paris, though we find him at Cherbourg at
different times. The good people had been
disturbed at his way of using the bounties

* Millet always said that the years 1843–44 were the hardest in
his life, when his first wife, dying, left him a widower and childless.

accorded, and gave him in 1841, perhaps as a test of his powers, the commission to paint the portrait of a deceased mayor. The work did not meet with their approval, they refused to accept it, and, it is said, even his old teacher, Langlois, abandoned him; but a few years later, in 1844, when a Salon picture had attracted considerable attention, Cherbourg gave him a better reception. He was even offered a professorship of drawing in the college, but wisely refused the position.

The struggle for existence during these years was at times a severe one. The little family was often on the verge of actual want, or even passed it. Thus Millet, receiving a hundred francs, brought him by a friend in 1848, said: "Thanks; they come in season. We have not eaten for two days; but the important thing is that the children have not suffered—they have had thus far their nourishment." He painted anything and everything asked of him ; *e. g.*, in Cherbourg in 1841, signs for a veterinary surgeon, a tight-rope dancer, a sail maker. The thirty francs he received for a sign painted for a midwife in Paris in 1848 supported him and his for fifteen days.

Diaz, who had formed a high opinion of his talents, was indefatigable in his efforts to secure him a patronage, as was Rousseau at a later period; and Sensier, who made his acquaintance in 1847, was thenceforward his devoted friend; but the comradeship among the few younger men who were loyal to him, while affording him a moral support, never kept want long or far distant.

Sensier mentions the prices he received for his pictures in 1848; six beautiful drawings for a pair of shoes, four portraits of Diaz, Barye, Victor Dupré and Vechte, life size to the bust, for twenty francs; any number of charming sketches, at prices ranging from five francs to one.

His art studies consisted chiefly in saturating himself with the spirit of the old masters, whom he had chosen as his guides. One who has known and loved Millet cannot walk to-day through the Louvre without recalling how he haunted it. Poussin's cool, strong landscape in the *Salon Carré*, the devout work of the child-masters of Italy in the long room beyond, and Michelangelo's drawings have a more intimate interest for us because of what they taught Millet.

But Millet had not yet reached entire self-consciousness. Perhaps it would be more true to say that he did not yet dare to be altogether himself, on account of the home which little ones were fast entering. He must earn money and therefore paint what could be sold. He had acquired remarkable facility. Sensier recalls walks in the fields (Montmartre or Saint-Ouen) at this time, and finding in his *atelier*, on the morrow, all the impressions of the outing as finished paintings. He was known among artists as the "Master of the Nude," that being the class of subjects wherein he had done most and his best work. Sensier says: "Until 1847, Millet painted external life, human nudity, in its most unconscious state, the purely physical life of beings that let existence flow past as the stream of oblivion. He did not paint the soul and its torments, as he did later, but living forms, and he depicted them with the alluring charm of material beauty, in their movements as well as in their repose."

To judge from his biographer's description, Millet's facility with his brush and the demands of life combined for a time to carry him to the limits of propriety. An ex-

MILLET

hibition at Havre in 1845 and a "Temptation
of Saint Jerome" of the same period represent this extreme phase. Reports thereof
awoke apprehension in the Gruchy home.
The good grandmother acted shrewdly here.
She did not upbraid her beloved foster-child,
but sent him a patriarchal exhortation.
"Follow the example of that man of your
own profession who used to say: 'I paint
for eternity.' For no cause whatever, permit
yourself to do evil works or to lose sight of
the presence of God. With Saint Jerome,
think incessantly that you hear the trumpet
that shall summon us to judgment."*

Millet always cherished a reverential love
for his grandmother, and never became
modern Parisian enough to have been in-
sensible to this appeal. "Millet had a
sensuous organization," Sensier says, "in love
with the flesh, but his soul was upright and
almost without a spot. In the midst of our
decadence, he has guarded the purity of a
primitive heart."

"The atmosphere of Paris was heavy to
him, the small talk, . . . the ambitions, the
morals, the fashions, threw him into a world

* Millet's father charged him, on his deathbed, "never to execute
a work of impiety, and that all his desire should be to praise God by
thought, word and deed."

[49]

he did not understand." The revolution of 1848 came. Millet, with all other citizens, had to shoulder a musket and defend the assembly. At the capture of the barricades of his quarter, Rochechouart, he saw the chief of the insurgents fall. That intensified his aversion to Paris. He had already sent two pictures to the Salon in 1848, one of which, *"Le Vanneur"* (a man winnowing corn), attracted attention. It was his first important attempt to paint a scene from farm life. Ledru-Rollin, the minister, purchased it for five hundred francs, and gave him a commission to paint another canvas for eighteen hundred francs. Millet chose for his subject "Hagar and Ishmael." It was a nude, and the work was almost done when he overheard a conversation between two young men, as he was passing one evening before the art store of Deforge. They were looking at his *"Baigneuses"* (Bathers). "Do you know the author of this picture?" one asked. The other replied: "Yes, it's a fellow called Millet, who only paints nude women."

On reaching home, Millet told his wife the story, and added: "If you wish, I will never again do any more of this painting;

Les Baigneuses

Les Baigneuses

life will be still harder, you will suffer from it, but I shall be free and shall accomplish that which has long occupied my mind." She replied simply: "I am ready; do according to your will." "Hagar and Ishmael" was left unfinished, and a second scene from peasant life, "The Haymakers Resting," took its place.

Millet had just received the pay therefor, when political troubles again broke out, the manifestation of the thirteenth of June, 1849; the cholera was also at its height. He decided therefore to abandon Paris for a time, and went, with his friend Jacque, to Barbizon.

Will Low describes charmingly the entrance of the peasant painter into that realm of labor he was to immortalize, and where he was to find his true self. Jacque, it seems, had heard of the quaint, tiny village on the borders of the great forest, but had forgotten all save the last syllable of its name, "zon." So the two families took the diligence from Paris through Chailly to Fontainebleau. Thence the brother artists explored the forest on foot, finding Barbizon at last, and entering it through the cow-gate. The following day, Millet drove with his wife and children to where the footpath left the highway for the village. Dismounting, the Norman peasant took his two little girls on his broad shoulders and trudged ahead, while the wife followed with an infant of a few months in her arms, a servant with a basket of provisions accompanying her. Rain fell, the mother's skirts had to be raised to shield the little one, and a peasant woman, noticing the bedraggled procession, took the Millets for strolling actors.

Their first home was at the village's western end, away from the forest. A peasant, proprietor of a cottage of two rooms, ceded one of them, and the other, which he himself occupied, served, with its fireplace, as kitchen and dining-room for both families. Millet's *atelier* was across the street. But Millet soon discovered, at the other end of the village, an unoccupied peasant house, one story and a loft in height, and this became his permanent home.* A garden, forty-eight feet wide, ran its entire length. A door in the high stone wall at the rear of

---

* The building was 61 feet long, 16 feet wide and 17 feet from ground to ridge-pole.

Millet's Studio—Interior

Millet's Studio—Interior

the garden admitted to the plain. The house contained three rooms on the ground floor. The one nearest the street had been used as a barn and was without floor, save the bare earth, to judge from William Hunt's account. It was rarely heated, and then only by burning straw. The entrance to it was from the street end, and a window, three feet square, admitted light. This room served Millet as *atelier*, and the two rear rooms, floored, plastered, and with rafter ceilings, as home.

Five years later, his proprietor transformed a barn across the garden into an *atelier*, by putting in floor and rafter-ceiling and cutting a large window and a door, opening toward the old home, and rented it to Millet. The old *atelier* became a part of the living-quarters, which were enlarged as time went on, a home which many children entered.* The father's hope, however, to have a home of his own, "a nest for his little toads," as he expressed it, was never realized.

Millet came to Barbizon expecting to linger only for a brief period, but remained there twenty-seven years, or until his death. The hamlet has been transformed and

* Piednagel says Millet had nine children.

Millet's home has not escaped; the house and garden have disappeared. The *atelier* externally is unchanged, but within has been dismantled.* Fortunately, word-sketches remain, drawn by his friends Sensier, Piednagel, Clarétie, Yriarte, William Hunt and others, and the son of the artist, Carl Bodmar, has preserved in photographs the garden, the house as seen from the court, from the street, and the street itself, as they were in Millet's time.

The French villages, upon the borders of the Forest of Fontainebleau, consist of low houses, built of stone and plaster, and white-washed. The whitewash takes on, with the years, the color of a lichen, and the red tiles of the roofs become a deep, dull bronze, fringed here and there with rusty moss. The houses, or the groups of structures which constitute the homesteads, have an exterior and relatively unattractive side turned toward the outer world, and an interior of court, or courts and garden, shut away by high walls over which no intrusive eye can look. Sometimes the main house

---

* Millet's *atelier* was very simply furnished with a few casts, the spoils from the woods and fields, his favorite books, and, in the corner, a heap of blouses, aprons, kerchiefs, etc., sun and weather stained and bleached. Blue was his favorite color.

The Street of Barbizon Showing Millet's
Studio and Home

The Street of Barbizon Showing Millet's
Studio and Home

turns an end or a broad side toward the
street and its wall forms part of the parapet
which protects the intimacy of the home life.
Millet's *atelier* turned its broad side to the
village street, his little house its end.

We have the photographs before us as
we write, and also the memory of the
street, seen but yesterday. Between the
atelier and the house, over the wall which
seems to have twice the height of the
peasant woman in the foreground, thick-
foliaged trees rise in a bouquet. Wayward
sprays of vines, that are growing luxuriantly
within, escape over the wall. Wander
anywhere along the streets of the Fontainebleau hamlets and you will find numberless
pendants to this picture. We have pulled
the cord and, as the bell jangles within,
someone admits us to the home world.
Piednagel describes the house as "a
maisonette literally covered with a thick
growth of clematis, ivy and jasmine of
Virginia. The little door, formerly painted
white and without any ornament, is never
closed to him who knocks. The façade of
this modest dwelling looks out upon a large
garden, all filled with an attractive disorder.
Flowers, vegetables, and fruits grow there

without any thought of symmetry and seem
to live and multiply in perfect intelligence.
A great white rose vine, inquisitive and
artful, seems to be trying to scale the
windows, and a hedge of sweetbrier and
elders, twined about with convolvulus, announces the beginning of the garden."

Nature was the only member of the
Millet household that had abundant stores
and could make therefore lavish expenditure.
But the French peasant knows how to make
this guest feel at home, giving her space
and freedom, and Millet had not merely
the peasant's love for foliage and flowers,
but the artist's sympathy with everything
that lives in Nature. Sensier says that he
loved Nature so that the pruning of the ivy
or the clematis caused him an actual pain.
Once, after returning from a walk in the
forest, resplendent, imperial in its frost
raiment, Millet attempted to describe the
scene. "The tiny branchlets of all kinds
were perhaps the most beautiful of all," he
said; "it seems to me that Nature wishes
to make them take their revenge and to
show that they are not inferior in anything,
those poor, humiliated things."

Jules Clarétie admits us to the interior

Millet's Garden—With Madame Millet

Millet's Garden—With Madame Millet.

of the house. "On the right side of the street, in going toward the forest, one can see around a table, lighted by a lamp, a family patriarchally grouped. The mother and the father are there, the children are working, the girls sewing. All are silent. Sometimes the father, who is reading to himself, finishes his reading aloud. They listen without raising their heads. The father is a large and robust man, young still, with gentle expression, calm and severe at the same time, with black beard, something of the peasant and of the Quaker. He is silent and usually dreaming."

Others paint equally beautiful home scenes. It is evening; Marian and George are standing near him, the youngest child is on his knees and Millet is humming a rustic ballad; or it is afternoon and he is strolling in the forest, a child among his children, weaving fantastic stories. The last time Sensier saw him free from suffering and happy, six months before his death, all went to the forest, Millet, his wife, Sensier, the children and the grandchildren. He was spoiled by all the members of his family, all noises were hushed near his studio, even the youngest remembering not to disturb

Papa at his work; but, when discouragement came, he threw the studio door wide open and forgot the disconsolate artist in the happy father.

If you leave the *atelier* behind and turn toward the forest, within five minutes you will be in an open grove with stately trees. To the right, as far as a startled pheasant will fly, on the face of a cleft boulder, forming one of an enormous, primeval heap, a bronze tablet has been inserted, containing heads of Millet and Rousseau. Fifteen minutes farther, either to the right or left, will lead to commanding platforms. The wood falls away to the west, and the plain, dotted with villages, is spread out as on a map.

A forest fire has recently swept the spaces just beyond, and many of the famous oaks that Millet knew and loved are black and grotesque shapes now. Within easy walking distance, however, not more than an hour from Barbizon, are the most beautiful portions of the forest. The *Bouquet du Roi* extends for a considerable distance, a narrow wood road, lined on both sides with stately trees that form a continuous, sloping roof through which the sunlight sifts. The

The Gleaners

forest stretches away, clear of underbrush,
or with enough left in spaces to afford a
marvelous contrast between the fresh green
of the bushes, the dark, grey trunks banded
with light, and the forest roof, a fretwork
of green leaves and blue sky, with the sunlight burning through it all. None but
the noblest trees may have place in this
park of the kings. The walk through it
in the late afternoon defies description.
The consciousness of beauty becomes actual
pain, through bewilderment and intensity.

Millet wrote: "If you could see how
beautiful the forest is! I run there sometimes, at the close of the day, after my day's
work is done, and I return therefrom always
crushed. I do not know what those beggars
of trees say to each other, but they say
something which we do not understand,
because we do not speak their language.
Voila tout!"

Overtaken by the close of day in the
gorges of Apremont, he exclaimed: "It is
a prehistoric deluge, a chaos. It must
have been terrible, when it ground under
its masses generations of men, when the
grand waters had taken possession of the
earth and only the Spirit of God survived

so many disasters. The Bible paints it in three words: '*Et spiritus Dei superabat super aquas.*' (And the Spirit of God prevailed over the waters.) Poussin alone, perhaps, has understood that end of the world."

The reverse of this picture of a happy home life and constant, intimate communion with Nature is the long, cruel struggle with poverty, headache and disappointment.* His letters show that the morrow scarce ever was secure. He was often in fear of being turned out of doors. About the time that his "Angelus" was finished he wrote to Sensier: "We have only wood for two or three days more . . . I am suffering and sad." William Hunt says: "I found him (Millet) working in a cellar, three feet under ground, his pictures becoming mildewed, as there was no floor. He was desperately poor, but painting tremendous

---

* Sensier's portrayal of Millet's struggle with poverty has been criticised, even by Madame Millet, as overdrawn. But Millet's letters seem to bear out at least the assertion that, in his mind, the situation was tense almost to the last, causing great solicitude, if not actual material want. All the responsibility therefor is not however to be imputed to lack of due appreciation of his work as artist. The needs of a very large family, with his generous shielding them against the suspicion even of distress, and his own lack of financial wisdom, his incautiousness when fortune smiled, were also contributory causes. His eldest son said they were the happiest of children and only knew later on that their father's life had been worn out by his hard struggle.

things." The most cruel part of it all, in the retrospect, is that the struggle was ended, his existence assured and hostile criticism stilled only about 1870, that is a few years before the end, when already the strong man was broken by the burden bearing.

In December, 1874, when he was consciously entering the shadow land, he said: "I die too soon; I disappear at the moment when I begin to see clear in nature and art." In January, 1875, a stag was pursued into a garden near by and tortured to death. Millet heard all. "It is a prognostic," he said; "that poor animal, which has just died near me, announces without doubt that I too am going to die." January 20th, 1875, the long struggle ended. At his death there was, as his biographer expresses it, an explosion of sympathy and justice. Whatever might be the variance of opinion with regard to his art interpretation, all recognized that a brave man had passed. Single canvases, that could scarce find a buyer at any price when first painted, have brought since his death prices that would have assured him not merely a competence, but wealth. Thus, "The Gleaners," which Millet had sold for two thousand francs, brought three hundred thousand francs; and "The Angelus," which he had great difficulty in disposing of for twenty-five hundred francs, brought, at the Secretan sale in 1889, five hundred and fifty-three thousand francs, and later, in 1890, eight hundred thousand francs. The Gavet collection of his pastels and drawings was sold in the year of his death for four hundred and thirty-one thousand francs.*

Yet this story is a common one, and the wish of his heart, despite all, had been fulfilled. For he wrote in 1867: "I continue to desire only this, to live from my work and to bring up my children fittingly; then to express the most possible of my impressions; also, and at the same time, to have the sympathies of those I love well. Let all this be granted me and I shall regard myself as having the good portion."

Millet's nature was saddened by the struggle. The cloud that hung forever in his sky dulled his vision to the im-

* High prices were realized at sales, even before his death. In 1873, "The Angelus," which was one of his favorites, sold for 50,000 francs; "Woman with the Lamp," 38,500; "Flock of Geese," 25,000; and others for corresponding prices; but Millet was already sick and had hemorrhages. The May following his death, his unfinished pictures, drawings, etc., sold for 321,000 francs and this gave Madame Millet a comfortable income. Proofs of etchings he had sold for half a franc brought from 100 to 150 francs.

The Angelus

portant part that light and gladness have in Nature, aye to the sunny side of that peasant life whereof he had always been a part and whose interpreter he felt himself called to be. Yet, despite money vexations, despite the demon headache, which gained a tighter clutch upon him every year and pitilessly stole away strength and time from creative work, despite his repeated failures to secure recognition, he walked manfully forward and, in the darkest years, wrought much of his noblest work.

About the time of his finishing "The "Gleaners" (in 1857) he said: "Let them not believe that they will force me to lessen the types of the soil; I would prefer to say nothing rather than to express myself feebly. Let them give me signs to paint; yards of canvas to cover by day's labor, as a painter of buildings; a mason's work, if need be; but let them leave me in peace to conceive, according to my own fashion, and accomplish my task." When his "Death and the Wood-chopper" had been refused at the Salon, in 1859, he said: "They believe that they will make me bend, that they will impose upon me the art of the Salons. Ah, No! Peasant I was born, peasant I shall die. I wish to say that which I feel. I have things to describe as I have seen them, and I will remain upon my soil without retreating a *sabot's* length, and, if need be . . . I will fight too . . . for honor."* From the misunderstanding and non-appreciation of man he turned constantly to Nature for cheer: "Let us go and see the sunset; that will comfort me again." When well nigh disheartened, in 1864, he wrote: "Let us pray Him who gives us intelligence not to abandon us too much, for we have need of all our strength to accomplish this task. Gird we up our loins, then, and march!"

Sensier visited Millet and Jacque frequently during the first months after they came to Barbizon, and found them so overwhelmed by the beauty of the forest that they could not work. The charm of forest and plain and the exhilarating consciousness of being at last free to live his own life combined for a time to intoxicate Millet. "When I get to the ground," he had said before leaving Paris, "I shall be free."

With the return of calm, he began his life work, sketching everything that spoke to him and working very rapidly in the

* "The Angelus" was already painted.

preparation of these first notes. Later he elaborated with care a series of small studies, embracing the entire life of the peasant, both man and woman, and almost from cradle to grave. His paintings, the final stage in this work of creation, grew slowly. He did not finish more than three a year. He was a severe and patient self-critic. If he felt the expression incomplete, he let the canvas hang untouched for months, even years. He did not paint from the model. He sought the typical rather than the individual, and the model would obscure the type that was taking form within.

We are accustomed to think of the Barbizon period as completely severed from the earlier period, in that the painting of the nude, wherein Millet had shown hitherto his chief mastery, was abandoned. But this is an error. He continued, for ten years still, 1848–58, producing nude studies, side by side with his peasant interpretations.

When it was known that Millet was to abandon Paris for Barbizon, Diaz, the lover of color and graceful form, protested. "What! In the name of the great pontiff, do you pretend to tell me that you have decided to live with brutes and sleep on weeds and thistles, to bury yourself among peasants, when, by remaining in Paris and continuing your immortal flesh painting, you are certain to be clothed in silks and satins?" Diaz expressed a truth with regard to Millet's nudes. Their strong and simple lines and their noble, sensuous forms declare him a master in this field. Millet's sketches afforded him the largest opportunity for the free exercise of that quality wherein he excels, the power to express form, character, motion with few, sure lines. In his large canvases expression does not always equal conception. Yet considering art "not for art's sake" alone, but as one of many fields of man's creative power that may contribute to the uplift of all life, Millet's peasant canvases remain his supreme achievement.

We learn, from Yriarte, that he removed a portion of his wall in order to have, almost on the level of the ground, a view out upon the country, and there, seated upon a heap of stones, passed hours in contemplation. Sensier tells us that his occupations at Barbizon were twofold,—in the morning he dug his garden, and after breakfast, that is in the afternoon, he retired to a low-roofed, cold, dark hall which he called his

A Sketch—Millet

studio. If he remained there too long, he would have frightful headaches which lasted perhaps for weeks. To ward them off, he wandered about the fields and forests in *sabots*, an old straw hat and an old sailor's blouse, and there his full vigor returned.

His work has been styled "The Poem of the Earth." Life was to Millet profoundly serious, permeated with the divine. Every act of life should be related to the eternal order of things; every work, well done, is so related. The church had taught him to leave the afar to God. The riddle of the near, he read as discipline. Through work shalt thou earn thy bread, and, more, become a part of the regenerative force that shall redeem the earth. He had found his place. His part, as God's servant, was to take page after page from the book of the fields about him and read it to his fellow-man.

The peasant's work is both the first and the most fundamental of human labors. Millet was close to the soil by birth and instinct. He felt rightly that, with the primer of peasant life, from which all complexities of higher social organization are absent, he could best contribute his part to

the interpretation of life—at least describe
soil and life-pictures, in their beauty and
strength, which the eye saw but the mind
apprehended not. By force of sincerity, he
related what he himself even did not fully
grasp. Submissive himself to earth's un-
equal allotment of good and evil, of the
rewards of labor, he pressed home with
such crude verity the fact of this inequality
that men began to think more seriously
thereof, and the readjustment of society, the
realization of human brotherhood, is being
advanced to-day by his work, without his
having sought or even dreamed of such a
result.

The Barbizon peasants were not unfortunate above other French peasants; nay,
more favored, for they were comparatively
well-to-do, with field and forest as store-
houses of food and heat. Millet recognized
this.* He was not portraying the Barbizon
peasant, nor even the peasant, as peasant, but
as symbol of humanity. The faces of his
peasants are not only not individualized,
but are usually without expression, often
wholly in shadow, or only suggested. That

* He said repeatedly that he did not consider the Barbizon
peasants unfortunate.

In the Fields—Barbizon

(From Nature)

is to us purposeful. Man even must in a measure be obscured, the God in his face veiled, if he who looks upon the canvas is to realize that humanity after all is only a part, though an important part, of a greater whole, only an instrument in the hands of Omnipotence.

When it was objected to his portrayals of peasant life that pretty maids and fine-looking men could be found in the village as well as in the city, and that he was calumniating the country by deliberately choosing the brutal and formless, he answered: "Beauty does not dwell in the face; it radiates forth from the whole figure and appears in the suitableness of the action to the subject. Your pretty peasants would be ill suited for picking up wood, for gleaning in the fields of August, for drawing water from a well. When I paint a mother, I shall strive to represent her beauty solely in the look she gives her child. Beauty is expression."

Elsewhere he interprets the same thought more clearly: "I would wish that the beings I represent should have the air of being consecrated to their position and that it should be impossible to imagine that the idea could occur to them of being other thing than that which they are." "One can say that all is beautiful which arrives in its time and at its place, and contrariwise. . . . The beautiful is the suitable." "One can start from all points in order to arrive at the sublime, and everything is proper to express it if one has a sufficiently high aim. Then that which you love with the most self-forgetting and passion becomes your beautiful . . . The entire arsenal of nature has been at the disposal of the strong men, and their genius has made them take there, not the things which men have agreed to call the most beautiful, but those which suited the place best. Has not everything, at every hour and in a certain place, its rôle? Who would dare to decide that a potato is inferior to a pomegranate?"

* "There are those who tell me that I deny the charms of the country. I find there far more than charms—infinite splendor. I see there, as they do, the little flowers of which the Christ said: 'I assure you that Solomon even in all his glory was never clothed like one of these.' I see

* This letter was written in reply to the criticisms of his "Man with the Hoe."

The Man with the Hoe

The Man with the Hoe

very well the aureoles of the dandelions, and the sun, which displays down there, far away beyond the villages, his glory in the clouds. I do not see the less on that account the laboring horses all steaming in the plain, then in a rocky place a back-broken man, whose *'hans'* (pantings) have been heard since morning, who is trying to straighten himself upright for a moment in order to breathe. The drama is en-veloped with splendors. That expression, 'The cry of the earth,' is not my invention; it was discovered long ago. My critics are men of education and taste, I imagine; but I cannot put myself in their place, and, as I have never seen in my life any other thing than the fields, I try to say as well as I can that which I saw and experienced when I worked there. Those who wish to do better have certainly the good por-tion."

"See those things which are moving down there in a shadow. They are creep-ing or walking, but they exist; they are the genii of the plain. They are nothing but poor folk, however. It is a woman all bent, without doubt, who is bringing back her load of grass; it is another, who is

[71]

dragging herself along exhausted under a bundle of fagots. From a distance they are superb. They square their shoulders under the burden, the twilight devours their forms; it is beautiful, it is grand as a mystery."

Paul Victor said of Millet's figures: "His painting of 'The Reapers' is an idyl of Homer translated into *patois*. His rustics . . . are of a superb, brutal, primitive ugliness, resembling the figures of captives sculptured on Egyptian tombs. . . . You feel a respect in the presence of those rude peasants, companions of the great cattle, warriors armed with scythes, nourishers of men."

*William Hunt said: "Millet's pictures have infinity behind them. His subjects were real people, who had work to do. If he painted a haystack it suggested life, animal as well as vegetable, and the life of man. His fields were fields in which men and animals worked, where both laid down their lives, where the bones of the animals were ground up to nourish the soil and the endless turning of the wheel of existence went on."

---

* Millet said once that Hunt was the best and most intimate friend he had ever had.

Sheep at Edge of Wood

Sheep at Edge of Wood

MILLET

Many looked upon Millet's peasants as hiding a political protest, breathing the spirit of social revolution. That heavy boor, scarce above the ox, his comrade in toil, painted on the cold canvas without any softening of lines, and thrust before the eyes of the delicately nurtured and well-clad, seemed the cry of the country against the city, of the toiler against the man of ease.* But nothing was farther from Millet's idea. His spirit knew not such a thing as protest against the ordering of God and Nature. Turning backward over the centuries, he heard the curse spoken. He felt its shadow brooding over all the earth, darkening the tilled field, bending the back of the laborer. It was a mystery, but to a Millet human toil and pain are but the discipline of divine justice, love and wisdom. His canvases present life as he saw it, reveal profound sympathy with toiling humanity, but breathe neither lament nor protestation.

He said repeatedly: "My programme is work, for every man is vowed to bodily fatigue: 'Thou shalt live in the sweat of thy brow' was written centuries ago, an im-

* When his "Sower" appeared at the Salon of 1850, one critic went so far as to see in it a Communist flinging handfuls of shot against the sky.

[73]

mutable destiny. . . . What every one ought
to do is to seek progress in his own profession, exert himself always to do better,
to become strong and noble in his occupation and to surpass his neighbor by talent
and conscientiousness in work. That is for
me the only path. . . ." In 1867 he wrote:
"I repel with all my strength the demo-
cratic side, as it is understood in the language
of the clubs, that they have wished to
attribute to me. My sole desire has been
to direct thought to the man consecrated to
earning his livelihood in the sweat of his
brow. . . . I have never had the idea of making any plea whatsoever, *Je suis paysan paysan.*" No fact in Millet's life is clearer
than that he was always remote in thought
and purpose from radicalism.*

Millet was as sensitive as any of his
contemporaries to the splendors of the
earth. "Ah! I would wish," he exclaimed, "I could make those who look
at what I do feel the terrors and the
splendors of the night. One ought to be
able to make the songs, the silences, the
murmurs of the air heard. One must per-

* He said often that he failed to grasp Socialist doctrines and
that all revolutionary principles were distasteful to his ideas. He
did not even read political newspapers.

ceive infinity. Is not one terrified when one thinks of those constellations of light which have risen and set for centuries upon centuries with a regularity nothing disturbs? They give light to everything, the joys and the sorrows of men, and when this world of ours shall sink, that sun, so beneficent, will be only a pitiless witness of the universal desolation." He says of winter: "Oh, sadness of the fields and woods, one would lose too much not to see you!" And elsewhere: "Oh, spaces which made me dream so when I was a child, will it never be permitted me to make you even suspected?" *

But his supreme interest was centred in man. "It is the human side which touches me most in art and, if I could do that which I wish, or at least attempt it, I would never create anything which was not the result of an impression received through the appearance of Nature, either in landscapes or figures. It is never the joyous side which presents itself to me. I do not know where it is, I have never seen it.

---

* He wished every canvas to suggest infinity. "Every landscape, however small, should contain a suggestion of the possibility of its being indefinitely extended on either side. Every glimpse of the horizon should be felt to be a segment of the great circle that bounds our vision."

The gladdest thing I know is the calm, the silence that one enjoys so deliciously, either in the forest or in the tilled fields, whether tillable or not. You will admit to me that it is always very dreamful there and the dream sad, though delicious. You are seated under the trees experiencing all the well-being, all the tranquility one can enjoy. You see coming forth from a little path a wretched form laden with fagots. The unexpected and always startling way in which that figure appears to you, carries you back at once to the sad condition of humanity, weariness. That gives always an expression analogous to that of La Fontaine in his Fable of the Wood Cutter:

'Quel plaisir a-t-il eu depuis qu'il est au monde?
En est-il un plus pauvre en la machine ronde?'

In the places that are tilled, though sometimes in certain regions scarce tillable, you see figures digging with spade or mattock. You see one of them from time to time straightening up his loins, as we say, and wiping his brow with the back of his hand. 'Thou shalt eat thy bread in the sweat of thy brow.' Is that there the gay, merry labor in which certain people would like

to make us believe? It is there, notwith-
standing, that I find the true humanity, the
grand poetry."

The peasant patiently bearing his burden
from the cradle to the grave, in the hot
fields of summer and the cold, desolate
woods of winter, was to Millet the earth
poem, and grander far than royal sunset or
voice of wind in the forest. There was the
battle of life out there in the fields. There
was the world's true hero, sowing, reaping,
gleaning. He was redeeming the earth
from its curse and making atonement, by a
life of self-renunciation, for the vast, primal
sin; waiting too patiently the revealing of
the world of peace and joy beyond. The
scintillation of the stars whispered to him
thereof as he watched by the sheepfold at
night. When as evening fell the Angelus
sounded forth from the bells of the village
church tower, he bowed his head and
drank in for a moment a holy, quiet peace,
presage of that beyond.

Such was the poem that formed itself in
Millet's mind; every action of the peasant
life, indoors and outdoors, takes on a religious aspect in his canvases. It is humanity performing the old necessary, patri-

archal services, man working with Nature, both under the shadow, under the burden, uncomplaining, waiting for the morning.

There is without doubt a deep truth in all this. That peasant and son of peasants in coarse blouse and *sabots* who roamed these woods so many years was one of the prophets. The forests of the Bas Bréau and the gorges of Apremont are holy places to-day, because Jean-François Millet walked there. And yet it is only a part of the whole truth. Neither Nature nor human life rest all under the shadow. And he who, as Corot, finds and interprets the sun-sprent beauty of the woods, who sees bright-colored forms dancing in the glades, whose heart is sensitive, responsive to the joy, the carols that breathe everywhere in this world, is a prophet too.

The life of the peasants has another side. Sunlight and song are not all reserved for that morrow of whose advent the stars murmur at night and the Angelus at sunset. Walk through these village streets. The houses stand sociably close to each other, not separated, as in a hamlet of the western world. It is evening; the fields of labor lie still and waiting under the stars.

Feeding the Nestlings
(La Becquee)

There are groups upon the streets and the neighborly talk has a cheery ring. Enter through the gate ajar and sit down with the peasant family in the open court, if it is midsummer, around their table. It is rudely, but generously spread. These men and women were at work with the sunrise and the day has but just ended for them. They are bent, perhaps, the oldest ones especially, but there is a gladness, a song in their greeting, in their voices, that tells not only of a kindly, social spirit, but also that Nature has not been altogether a harsh stepmother to them.

No, the life of humanity is not all under the shadow; it is earnestness, it is unceasing effort, it is tireless aspiration, if a true life; but song and sunshine are as integral a part of it as sorrow and cloud. The trees rise grey and tall about me, and the wind is soughing in their upper branches, but the sunlight is filling all the forest world with sparkle and shimmer, the birds are chattering overhead; a roe-buck took my place yesterday beneath the beech tree, when I had deserted it for the noon hour.

Each poet-painter sings his measure, each

prophet declares that part of the whole truth revealed to him. But the whole envelops the parts and reaches outward into the infinities. And we who listen to these partial truths begin at last to hear, as sound of distant bells, the disclosings of the whole truth.

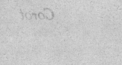

Corot

Corot

In the Fields
(*Sketch after photo.*)

Corot

TAKE the train at the Saint-Lazare station for Ville-d'Avray. The road, after tunnelling Paris and traversing the nearer suburbs, crosses the Seine and makes a broad sweep, climbing and following the high ground that encircles as a ring the basin through which the river winds. The backward and downward look is inspiring. The great city lies just beneath, with the Eiffel Tower far overtopping everything, the Arc de Triomphe and the turrets of the Trocadéro Palace as conspicuous objects in the foreground. The sun has set aflame a gilded ball far back among the swarming myriads of structures, the overflow from Lutecia, the tiny island city of Roman times. To the left rise the heights of Montmartre, surmounted with the white, unfinished church. A fortressed hill is near, " a watch-dog of Paris," as Hugo calls it. Then the Bois de Boulogne comes between, and the Seine winds at the foot of the ridge, with low trees, trimly uniformed, sentinelling its banks. Groups of tall, gaunt Lombardy

poplars stand here and there in the file, like
survivors of a sturdier militia.

There are villas everywhere. The Frenchman, who loves the country and yet would
not be out of sight and hearing, out of near
reach, of the bright, gay capital, can pitch
his stone tent upon the terraces of this ridge
and see the lights of the city and its
suburbs, swarming multitudinous down into
the valley, the flight of a song away, while
taking his evening meal *en famille* in his
own pretty, vine-roofed arbor.

We pass Saint-Cloud, rush in and out of
tunnels and are at Sèvres-Ville-d'Avray.
Sèvres is below on the river, but Paris and
the Seine are hidden. Ville-d'Avray is
farther back on the ridge. We saunter
hillward, following the Chemin Corot, the
channel through which the daily tide of
city travel ebbs and flows. There are villas
on both sides. To the left green vines
wanton along high stone walls, dropping
here and there a fresh spray, and behind
rise trees luxuriantly foliaged.

We have reached the Avenue de Versailles, the main thoroughfare of Ville-
d'Avray, and turn to the left. There are
gates invitingly open on the valley side,

glimpses of flower gardens and parks, of a downward sweep of lawn and an upward climb beyond, that allure almost to intrusion. Then we are in a *bourgeois* part of the town; the houses are in blocks, but between them, occasionally, a narrow space, an open door for our eyes, that wander eagerly down into that valley of mystery.

At last there is a break in the line, a broad open space, from which steps lead downward. We descend the steps and are at once on the shore of a small, beautiful lake. Water is gurgling from a marble fountain just at the foot of the steps. The fountain, surrounded by flower beds and overarched by trees, faces the tiny lake. It consists of a large, thick slab with triangular cornice, a base, and, in front, an urn to receive the water. A bird is singing on a branch in the cornice. A heavy laurel wreath, caught at the upper corners of the slab, falls in a festoon, and in lieu of a knot below there is a grotesque head, out of whose mouth water is flowing. Below the cornice is the inscription: "Veri diligentia" (Search after truth). A large medallion head has been cut in the slab, and beneath it we read: "Corot, Jean-Baptiste-Camille; born

at Paris July 26th, 1796; died at Paris
February 23d, 1875."

Opposite the fountain, across the path that
descends from the main street, a substantial
country house hides behind densely branched
trees and a high stone wall. It was Corot's
home, and nothing, we are told, has been
changed since his time. The house is
massive, of stone and plaster, a spacious,
old-fashioned home. Opposite the house
are the stables and outbuildings. Vines
run riot over them. House and stables look
at each other across an ample court. Beyond the enclosure, we catch glimpses of a
flower, fruit, and kitchen garden. It is a
picture of home comfort, of ease without
excess, taste without tinsel, with the quaint
flavor of olden times, the bright gladness of
flowers, the wild freedom of green vines and
rest beneath wide-branching trees.

But the door of the court is closed upon
us, so we follow the path past the house end
and study the garden over the high stone
wall and through the lattice work of the
foliage, left happily incomplete by Nature.
A bosky grove—a towered arbor—a broad
brook gliding between low-swung branches
—a marble statue hiding in a shady nook—

great trees rising everywhere—open spaces of sunlight.

As we turn and face the lake—we are at its foot now—we are amazed at the revelation. There are Corot's trees! Willows, more silvery leafed than any we have ever seen before, stand in sparse groups upon the bank, with tall, dark-green beeches between, and here and there a silver poplar; and on the opposite shore tall, gaunt trees, Lombardy poplars, with scarce any foliage, only a ragged ruffle of leaves twined about their stems.

It is a day of moods; while we linger, the sky becomes overcast and gray and the silver of the willow leaves is fused into a mist. The sun comes out for a moment and sets, in the distance, the facets of the lake sparkling. These are all familiar things, so familiar that we return and stand beneath Corot's windows. The ragged-foliaged poplars cannot be seen, but the silver willows are looking across, and the whole background is filled with the trees of the park climbing a gently sloping hill.

We saunter about the lake, make the acquaintance of the individual trees, look again at the genial face in the medallion, and then sit down before the whole, while the senses link in one all the separate impressions. Then we return by the grand hill-balcony of the railroad.

We have been looking forth upon scenes as familiar to Corot as the walls of his *atelier*. If the human element be eliminated, there is no pathos here, only loveliness everywhere, reaching its highest expression on the shores of the lake and within that jealously guarded court. Yet humanity is not only here in Corot's world but holds a larger place therein by far than in the villages upon the border of Millet's forest. The great city that camps in the plain has multitudes working harder, suffering more than ever Barbizon peasant. They bear life's burden with equal courage and patience. The fields of labor, that skirt the forest of Fontainebleau, have scarce other memories than those of man's tenacious, bloodless wrestlings with Nature. The teeming plain that surrounds that Seine islet has seen other steel flashing than that of hoe and ploughshare. A bloodier sweat than that of toil has dripped into its furrows. How can humanity be eliminated from a scene where it has been intensely, sufferingly active ever since the dawn of history?

The city laborer is lost in his environment; the eye perceives from that hill-balcony Nature and man's work, but not man. The graceful lines and grouping of park, river and hills, the grandeur and variety of architectural forms, the beauty, symmetry, and power of the city as a whole conceal from us the individual man.

The peasant stands alone in his fields, a statue of labor, hewn in the living flesh and freed in space, against the brown of the soil, the green of the meadows and woods, the blue of the sky. A still infinity surrounds him.

Millet's nature was in full sympathy with his environment, Corot's with his; but neither understood the other. Millet said: "Corot's pictures are beautiful, but they do not reveal anything new." Corot said of Millet: "His painting is for me a new world, I do not feel at home there. I am too much attracted to the old. I see therein great knowledge, air, and depth, but it frightens me; I love better my little music."

Beside every one of Millet's rugged, Dantesque strophes of toil should hang one of Corot's summer idyls, for each interprets only a part of Nature and life, and without the other is incomplete.

Jean-Baptiste-Camille Corot was born in Paris the 26th of July, 1796. His parents were milliners, then greatly in vogue, and their store was on the corner of the Rue du Bac and the Quai Voltaire, facing the Pont Royal. Here the young Corot was born. Thurwanger, his godson, says of his relation to his parents: "He had great respect for his father, but a real veneration for his mother, whom he considered the most beautiful of women. Unless away on a journey, he never failed, until his mother's death, to accompany her to church every Sunday. He was proud to walk with her, arm in arm, and always called her 'la belle femme.'" His father's family came from the vineyards of Burgundy. Corot discovered late in life some distant kinsfolk still living there, and, about 1860, went to visit them. He used to say to his friends later: "The country is full of good workers, who have the same name as myself; they call out to each other in the fields: 'Hé Corot!' You don't hear anything else. I always thought they were asking for me, and it seemed to me that I was there as in my own family."

Corot was proud of his peasant stock and had much of the peasant too about him, both physically and morally. Dumesnil describes him. "Of good height, strong, of a robust constitution, with a healthful, frank, jovial expression; liveliness and tenderness in his glance; a tone of *bonhomie*, blended with much penetration; great mobility of face and a ruddy complexion, which gave him the appearance of a peasant from the vineyards of Burgundy." His father sent him about 1806, for economical reasons, to the Lycée of Rouen, where he remained seven years, receiving there his entire education. While in Rouen, he was under the oversight of a correspondent of his father, a man of rather sombre tastes, who loved solitude and twilight walks. Young Corot used, therefore, to wander with him, usually toward sunset, in unfrequented paths, under the great trees of the meadows or along the river, and received from these solitary walks a profound impression.

His father intended to make of him a business man. After his return from Rouen, he was therefore placed in a draper's store, and remained in similar employ until about 1822. The artistic tendencies of his nature were already manifest. While working in the Rue de Richelieu, the moment he was at liberty he would hide himself under the counter and sketch. His employer was very indulgent, but told the father that the son would never be good for anything as a business man and he ought to let him follow his natural tastes.

Corot attributed to this business training his lifelong habits of order and punctuality. It was his custom always to rise early and, from the moment of his awakening, fix his thoughts upon the picture he was painting. He sang, Dumesnil says, while dressing, then ran to his easel, reaching his *atelier* promptly, summer and winter, at three minutes before eight.

Corot's father purchased in 1817 a country house in the Ville-d'Avray, the one we have described.* The family spent their summers there. Dumesnil says: "This dwelling was situated near a pond, . . . and often, while all were sleeping, he (Corot) remained in his room a part of the night, leaning upon the open window, absorbed in the contemplation of the sky,

*Corot and his sister occupied it together after their father's death.

Ville d'Avray

the water, and the trees. The solitude was complete; no noise came to trouble the dreamer on that solitary slope; he passed thus long hours, his eyes, and doubtless his thought, transported into that atmosphere, charged with humidity, impregnated with a kind of visible dampness composed of light and transparent vapors, which rose above the water. The souvenirs of his childhood and the impressions he had received at Rouen were thus renewed and implanted themselves more deeply in his brain. He attributed to them a great influence over his manner of seeing and feeling Nature, and over all his career as artist. From the moment that he took the brush, he found again, without difficulty, and as if unconsciously, the tones proper to express that which had remained in his imagination—that gray mist, light and ambient, wherewith the air is saturated, which half veils the horizons . . . in a majority of his paintings."

These are the years, in the growth of the human plant, when the senses of an artistically endowed nature open to the beautiful, as the petals of the convolvulus to the sunlight, and the whole course of a life may be determined by the slope of the hills, the sweep of the meadows, the aspects of environing nature. Corot's father had therefore chosen without due forethought in admitting Camille to this school of the Ville-d'Avray, where a sympathetic teacher was ever quickening his artistic senses and, in equal measure, deepening his aversion to commercial life.

He made, while a draper's clerk, the acquaintance of Michallon, the first recipient of the *Grand Prix de Rome*, a young man of his own age, and already highly esteemed. Michallon doubtless encouraged him in his ambitions. The yearning to express what he saw and felt became at last too strong for him to continue passively longer in the career his father had chosen for him. So one day he went to his father and begged him for permission to give up business, follow his natural inclination, and take the brush, "for that was what he most desired in the world."

Corot was then about twenty-six, yet his relation to his parents remained through life that of a child. Charles Blanc says that they always treated him as a little boy, and until after fifty he was as submissive to them as a child. The father, a shrewd business man, accustomed to command, was not pleased at this unwise choice; yet he did not, as he might have done, coldly thwart Camille's ambition. Probably the advice of Camille's employer and his own experience convinced him that his son would make a failure in business, unless he renounced now, for good and all, his art whims. He therefore resolved to give him a choice; to hold out before him a stimulating prospect, should he continue in business; but allow him if he wished, on meagre conditions, to follow his inclinations. He said: "The dowries of your sisters have been ready for them, and I expected very soon to provide you also with a good establishment; for you will speedily be of an age to be the head of a business house; but, since you have refused to continue in your trade, in order to become a painter, I forewarn you that, while I live, you will have no capital at your disposal. I will give you an allowance of fifteen hundred livres (francs). Never count upon anything else, and see if you can get along with that."* Camille, deeply

---

* That sum represented the interest of the dowry of one of his sisters, which had reverted to the family, she having died without children.

moved, embraced his father saying, "I thank you; it is all that I need, and you make me very happy."*   Forthwith delaying only long enough to provide himself with the tools of his new trade, he went down upon the shore of the Seine, close to his father's house and, "looking toward the Cité, full of joy, began to paint."†

This was Corot's first study, and he used to show it to all who visited his *atelier*. He said to Dumesnil, Français, Troyon, and Busson in, 1858: "While I was doing that, thirty-five years ago, the young girls who worked at my mother's were curious to see Monsieur Camille at his new employment, and ran away from the store to come and look at him.   One of them, whom we will call Mademoiselle Rose, came oftener than her companions; she is still living and unmarried, and visits me from time to time.   She was here only last week. Oh, my friends, what a change, and what reflections it calls forth!   My painting has not budged, it is as young as ever, it marks the hour and time of day when I made

---

*We have followed here Dumesnil's account. Charles Blanc says his father offered to put one hundred thousand francs in his hands, if he would continue in business. Thurwanger says the annuity was only 1,200 francs.

† The Seine island, site of the original city.

it; but Mademoiselle Rose and I, where
are we?"

The contrast between Millet's abandon-
ment of the farm and Corot's release from
the counter is a significant one. Millet's
father and grandmother saw, in the lad's
talent, a sign of the divine will, and sent him
forth, as one called to a higher, a holy
work. Corot's father had no confidence in
his son's artistic ability. The life of a
painter, at least so far as Camille was
concerned, seemed to him a half-idling,
a toying with life, and his attitude thenceforth toward his son was one of tolerance of
a caprice, rather than encouragement of a
talent.* Millet married, and his career was
from beginning to end a struggle, a consecrated one, from the moment of his clear
recognition of his special field. Corot
escaped from the counter to the land of his
dreams. He never married; whether the
desire thereof came to him or not, we are
not told—Mademoiselle Rose awakens a
suspicion—but, if it did, he turned his face

* Even so late as 1846, when Corot had been decorated with the
Legion of Honor, his father said to Français, who was perhaps Corot's
favorite pupil: "Tell me, you who are a connoisseur in painting,
whether Camille has really merit?" Français assured him that his
son was "stronger than all the rest," but found it difficult to con-
vince him.

resolutely away. He gave his life entirely to art; his father's allowances satisfied his modest needs, and so he lived on, interpreting Nature as she appeared to him, diffusing about him a constant sunshine, with a song always in his heart and upon his lips, until, dreaming of landscapes and skies all rose, he fell asleep.

When some one remarked that painting was a folly, he replied: "It may be so, but I defy anybody to find on my face the traces of sorrow, of ambition or remorse, which mar the faces of so many unhappy people. This is why we should not only pardon that folly but seek it. We should love art, which gives calm, moral contentment, and even health to one who can bring his life into harmony with it."

He said once to a friend: "I pray every day the *bon Dieu* to make me a child, that I may see her (Nature) as she is, and to make her, as a child, without reserve." Such prayers the *bon Dieu* always answers, for the desire is proof that the heart is open to receive the simple messages of the outer world, though not indeed its depths and heights; for these are only disclosed to him who has struggled and suffered. One may indeed suffer and yet remain a child. A mere financial independence, such as Corot enjoyed, is not a shield against the arrows of fate. But, so far as we can observe, Corot's life moved forward, from the time of his release from business, as evenly and happily as it is reasonably possible for human life to do. His vigorous health and glad nature, more receptive of sunlight than of shadow, counted for much therein. The failure to secure recognition had not the meaning for him that it had for Millet and Rousseau, harassed by creditors and dependent upon the fruits of their labors. It was therefore without that drop of supreme bitterness. Late in life, when the battle was over, he said, in reference to a suggestion made by Barye that he should offer himself as candidate to the Institute: "No," pointing to his easel, "all my happiness is there. I have followed my path without flinching, without changing, and for a long time without success; it has come late; it is a compensation for youth flown away, and I am the happiest man in the world."

His friend Michallon became for a brief time his teacher. His first drawing from nature was made at Arcueil under Michallon's eye.* Dumesnil sums up the precepts of his first master: "To come face to face with Nature, to strive to render her with exactness, to paint what one sees and to translate the impressions received," and this advice, Dumesnil adds, was about that which Corot gave in turn to his pupils. Though Corot did not remain long under Michallon's direction, the precepts of his first master had undoubtedly an abiding influence with him. They responded to the leadings of his own nature. Michallon died in 1822. His death must have occurred therefore not long after Corot's release from business.

René Ménard says of Michallon: "At a time when only conventional landscape was known, with the inevitable temple in the background, and the foreground with large leaves to give it distance, Michallon was regarded as a seeker after realism, because his subjects were chosen from Nature, instead of being composed in the imagination."

Victor Bertin, the acknowledged master of landscape, was Corot's second teacher. He had been also the teacher of Michallon.

---

* Corot made one of his first studies in the Forest of Fontainebleau, October 22d, 1822.

Dumesnil says that "he was a pure classicist, putting everything in order, and whose
paintings recall, if one may so express it,
the coldness of the accessories of tragedy."
Bertin was not the master to appreciate and
foster the artistic qualities of Corot's nature, but he was a conscientious worker
and a good draughtsman, and his instruction
was helpful in the direction of precision.

Jean Rousseau describes the ruling art
ideals at the time when Corot began his
apprenticeship. There was nothing but the
noble style; "no rivers, but torrents; no
houses, but Greek temples; no peasants,
but shepherds and nymphs; and no familiar
trees even, no simple elms and commonplace
birches, but cedars and palms."

After two winters spent in Bertin's studio,
Corot went to Rome in 1825. A number
of young French painters were there at the
time. Pierre Guérin was director of the
Academy. Corot's social qualities made at
first a much greater impression than his
ability as an artist. At the evening gatherings, at the Caffè della Lepre or Caffè Greco,
he used to sing with great gusto a ballad
then very popular, and which remained
one of his favorites,

" Je sais attacher les rubans,
Je sais comment poussent les roses.
Des oiseaux, je sais tous les chants,
Mais je sens palpiter mon coeur."

As an artist Corot was timid, and the indifference of his comrades went at times even to the point of ridicule. His first attempts at independent drawing discouraged him, and he felt that the time passed under Victor Bertin's instruction had been wasted. But he persevered and learned to sketch rapidly the groups he met on the street, seizing the character and the details too, if those who were unconsciously posing lingered long enough.

Corot, as Millet, was a more apt pupil in the large studio where Nature teaches than in the routine of the *atelier*. He loved to wander alone about Rome.*

Corot is indeed the child of the Ville-d'Avray and of Rome, the pupil of Nature and of Classic Art. He unites harmoniously the academic traditions taught by Michallon, Bertin and the rest, with his own impressions received immediately from Nature.

* There was no other city in Europe, even as late as 1875, save Athens perhaps, where one could learn as much of art and history by simply wandering to and fro. Rome was still ancient Rome, now it is an emerging modern European capital, and the crumbling gray of the old contrasts harshly with the pretentiousness of the new.

Souvenir of Castelgandolfo

For those lithe, shapely figures that lead
the dance in his summer landscapes are the
wood and river goddesses of ancient art,
most charmingly bereft of all heroic or
superhuman qualities, and become but the
impersonations of the hour and the mood of
Nature in color, in form, in posture, in
everything.

A comrade, Aligny, found him sitting one
day on the Palatine hill and sketching the
Coliseum. Aligny was regarded as an
authority in landscape. He was struck by
the precision of the sketch and, examining
it closely, discovered therein qualities of the
highest order, mastery and *naïveté* combined, and congratulated Corot. Corot at
first took this praise for pleasantry, but
Aligny insisted and told their comrades
that evening that Corot could well become
the master of them all. That gave Corot
a standing among his fellows and he was
thenceforth looked upon as an artist with a
future. Corot always attributed to Aligny
the success of his life. That spontaneous
recognition of his talent and hearty encouragement, coming from a man whose
judgment all respected, opened to him
again the golden gate. He made sketches

from nature at Aligny's advice, striving to render everything he saw with truth and precision, leaving no place to the imagination.

Charles Blanc says that Aligny exercised for fifteen years and more a powerful influence over Corot. During this period Corot "sought style by the drawing, by grand lines resolutely marked, an intentional sobriety in details. . . . That however which was rude, solemn and somewhat emphatic in the drawings of Aligny and in his virile, austere paintings . . . appeared in Corot less abrupt, more penetrated with the warmth of life. . . . Corot had something more than Aligny and Victor Bertin, and that was love. Everything depicted itself in harmony in his awakened soul."

Corot would never part with that study of the Coliseum, and toward Aligny he cherished always a reverential feeling. A friend whom Corot took to Aligny's studio, after Corot himself had become famous, was surprised to see him timid and as it were like a little boy in the presence of him whom he regarded as his true master.

Dumesnil describes the closing scene of that friendship. It was eight in the morning of a winter's day, the snow was falling and melting as soon as it touched the earth, the sky wan and sad. Aligny's funeral was being celebrated at Montparnasse. There were few present. Corot, then seventy-eight years old, stood shivering beside the grave. Madame Aligny came to him and begged him to go away, but he refused. Somewhat later that same day, as he was leaving his *atelier*, he related his experiences to Dumesnil. Just then a ray pierced the mist. "Ah," exclaimed Corot, "it's better weather now than it was this morning in the cemetery, but it was for me a duty, a sacred debt."

Edward Bertin, another of the French artists then at Rome, Aligny and Corot used often to wander about the Campagna together seeking *motifs*, and Corot said: "it was Edward who always had the instinct to choose the right spot." He felt he owed much to his counsels. Corot's first manner of painting, "dry rather than vaporous, has its source in the studies that he made at this time."

On Corot's return to France in 1827,* he sent two pictures to the Salon, and from that time forward never missed an exposition.

* He revisited Italy twice, in 1833 and 1843.

Yet it was long before he secured recognition His pictures were always badly hung, unnoticed by the critics, and returned unsold to him.* But he had, in compensation, from an early period a small band of admirers and champions, among others Diaz, and many warm friends, and was spared the bread struggle.

Charles Blanc says that "his work at first was idyllic or historic landscape, and did not differ enough from the work of his masters and the painters of the day to attract attention. Furthermore, the true sentiment of rustic nature was not yet awakened in the French school. When, a few years later, Cabat, Jules Dupré and Rousseau appeared, "the veil of mist and poetry which the amiable Corot had thrown over Nature was rent by that brilliant young group. The paintings of Corot seemed pale, gray, and, in their delicacy, they could attract only the delicate." These however were touched, and recognized therein the soul of a poet. We have seen but few of his earlier canvases. "The Coliseum" and "The Forum" in the

---

* He used to return sometimes from an exposition with tears in his eyes and look at the studies on the walls of his *atelier* saying: "At least they will not be able to take that away from me, with all their intrigues."

Un Paysage

Un Paysage

Louvre, dating from this first period, lack
that romance and that silver mist wherein
Corot found his natural expression, and they
disclose no other quality which separates
them from the throng.

Corot's " Paysage " in the Louvre seems
the natural and complete expression of the
life and spirit of the artist. A lake rests in
the silver haze of a summer morning. We
have often seen that gauze, woven of
minutest pearls, suspended over an Adiron-
dack lake. It is so tenuous that the eye
can pierce through its meshes to the shore
far away, and there, in the distance, the sun
has rent it, and on the glassy surface drops
of sunlight are falling and bursting.

The wooded shores are half shrouded in
mystery, half revealed. There is a life
stirring at this hour. Were the eye not so
dull, it would perceive graceful forms moving
rhythmically along the shore and among
the trees, or disporting themselves in the
lake. The ancients were not at fault when
they peopled lake and forest with nymphs
and dryads. For these were elusive things,
and the beauty of the woods and lakes, of
hours and moods such as this, has the same
elusive quality. But we turn back from

Nature to the "Paysage," or better, to its companion canvas, "Le Matin." There they are; Corot has seen them and painted them to the life—graceful, shapely, lithe, not mortal nor sensuous, as in the nude canvases of the modern school; not divine, nor heroic; of the woodland these; and how wonderfully the colors of their drapery blend with the tones of the landscape.

There is poetry everywhere, but it cannot speak the language of man until it has found an interpreter. And those beings, not of human, nor yet of heroic, divine kinship that Corot perceived and painted, are just and true impersonations of sentiments that exist in Nature, and without them his landscapes would lack their final perfection.

Corot recognized that he was not painting grand things.* "When I find myself in the fields," he said once to Silvestre, "I fly into a rage with my pictures." When standing before a painting of Delacroix, he exclaimed: "He is an eagle; I am only a skylark; I send forth little songs in my gray clouds." His remark about Millet's work, as compared with his own, voices the same thought.

* He said of his painting: "I know well that I do not go far in it; I cannot; but I am persuaded that I am on the right path."

Le Matin—Dance of the Nymphs

Le Matin—Dance of the Nymphs

Dumesnil finds in his religious paintings, the best of which are in Saint-Nicolas-du Chardonnet at Paris, a capacity for the grand art as represented by Titian, Poussin, Rembrandt and their fellows. But Corot would have deprecated such a comparison, and his own more modest judgment as to his distinctive place in art is the one time will approve.

We can spend a day with Corot by reading his letter to Monsieur Graham.

"Look you, it is charming, the day of a landscapist. He rises early, at three in the morning, before the sun; he goes and seats himself at the foot of a tree. He watches and waits. There is not much to be seen at first. Nature resembles a whitish canvas upon which the profiles of certain masses are vaguely sketched; all is fragrant, all thrills under the freshening breath of the dawn.

"Bing! the sun is becoming clear—the sun has not yet rent the gauze behind which hide the meadow, the valley, the hills of the horizon—The vapors of night still creep like silvery tufts over the cold, green grass. Bing! Bing! a first ray of the sun! a second ray of the sun! The tiny flowerets seem to awake joyous; each one has its drop of trembling dew; the leaves, sensitive to the cold, move to and fro in the morning air—Under the foliage the birds sing unseen—It seems as if it were the flowers saying their prayers. The loves, on wings of butterflies, descend upon the meadow and make the tall grasses sway to and fro. One sees nothing—everything is there—the landscape is all there behind the transparent gauze of the mist, which rises, rises, rises, inhaled by the sun, and discloses in rising the river scaled with silver, the meadows, the trees, the cottages, the vanishing distance. One distinguishes at last that which one divined at first.

"Bam! the sun has risen. Bam! the peasant passes at the end of the field with his cart drawn by two oxen. Ding! ding! it's the bell of the ram that leads the flock. Bam! bam! all bursts—all glitters—all is in full light, blond and caressing as yet. The distances, simple in contour and harmonious in tone, lose themselves in the infinity of the sky across an air misty and touched with azure. The flowers uplift their heads; the birds flit hither, thither. A countryman, mounted upon a white horse, disappears in the hollow path; the little rounded willows seem to be spreading themselves like peacocks upon the bank of the river. It is adorable, and I paint—and I paint—Oh! the beautiful fawn-colored cow, sunk up to her dewlap in the damp grass; I am going to paint her—crac! there she is! Famous, famous! *Dieu*, how well I've hit her off! Let's see what that peasant will say who is watching me paint and does not dare to approach. 'Ho, Simon!' Good; here is Simon approaching and looking. 'Well, Simon, what do you think of that?' 'Oh, well, Monsieur, it's very beautiful, of course (*Oh dom, M'sieu, c'est bien biau, allez!*)' 'And you see well what I meant to paint?' 'Why, of course, I see what it is; it's a large yellow rock you've put there.'

"Boom! boom! noon! the sun aflame burns the earth. Boom! everything grows heavy, everything becomes serious—the flowers hang their heads, the birds are silent, the sounds of the village come to us; they are the heavy labors, the smith whose hammer resounds upon the anvil. Boom! let us return home—One sees everything; there is nothing there longer. Let us go and breakfast at the farm, a good slice of home-made bread, with butter freshly churned — eggs, cream, ham — Boom! Work, my friends, if you will; I rest, I take my noon nap—and I dream a morning landscape—I dream my picture—by and by I will paint my dream.

"Bam! Bam! The sun sinks towards the horizon—It is time to return to work. Bam! the sun gives a blow of tamtam. Bam! it sets amidst an explosion of yellow, of orange, of fire red, of cherry, of purple—Ah, it's pretentious and vulgar; I don't like that—Wait; let's sit down there at the foot of the poplar—close to that pond, as smooth as a mirror.

"Nature has a tired mien—the flowerets seem to revive a little—poor flowerets, they are not like the rest of us men, who find fault with everything. They have the sun on the left—they are patient. 'Good,' they say to themselves, 'presently we'll have it on the right'—They are thirsty— they wait. They know that the sylphs of the evening are going to sprinkle them with vapor from their invisible watering pots; they wait in patience, giving thanks to God.

"But the sun sinks more and more behind the horizon. Bam! Bam! it casts its last ray, a smoke of gold and purple which fringes the fleeing cloud. Now then see! it has altogether disappeared! Good! Good! the twilight begins.

"*Dieu*, how charming it is! The sun has disappeared—There remains in the softened sky only a vaporous tint of pale lemon, the last reflection of that charlatan of a sun, which melts into the deep blue of night in passing through the greenish shades of pale turquoise, of a fineness unheard of, a delicacy fluid and intangible. The fields lose their color—the trees only form brown or gray masses—the darkened waters reflect the soft tones of the sky—One begins to see nothing more— one feels that everything is there—All is vague, confused. Nature is falling asleep —Yet the fresh air of the evening sighs among the leaves; the birds, those voices of the flowers, repeat the evening prayer— The dew strews with pearls the velvet of the lawn—The nymphs flee, hide themselves—and desire to be seen.

"Bing! a star of heaven plunges head foremost into the pond. Charming star,

[113]

whose scintillation the trembling of the water increases; you are looking at me—you are smiling at me and winking too—Bing! a second star appears in the water, a second eye opens. Welcome, fresh and smiling stars. Bing! bing! bing! three, six, twenty stars, all the stars of heaven have given each other a tryst in that blessed pond. All grows still darker—Only the pond scintillates—It is a swarming of stars. The illusion is produced—The sun having hidden itself, the inner sun of the soul, the sun of art rises—*Bon! Voila mon tableau fait!*" And afterward—

"After my excursions I invite Nature to come and pass several days with me. Brush in hand, I hunt for nuts in the forest of my *atelier*. I hear there the birds singing, the trees trembling under the wind. I see there the brooks flowing, and the river charged with a thousand reflections of the sky and of all that lives upon the banks—the sun rises and sets *chez moi*."

Corot, painted by himself, in the open-hearted abandon of correspondence, was a simple child, whose life fed upon the sunlight and the song of Nature, just as all green things that live in the forest do.

Life's sorrows and disappointments he knew unquestionably; for who can pass through life and not know them? Summer does not rule in Nature throughout the twelve-month, and even midsummer's shield cannot ward off the blow and gloom of the storm. Yet there are hearts, as there are fountains, so pure and self-nourished, that no shadow or soil of earth can tarnish them long. The returning sunlight chases the shadows away, the broken twigs and dead leaves, cast therein by the wind, are washed up on the bank, the impure dust lies clear at the bottom of the pool.

So it was with Corot; and the more we know about him, the more complete becomes the correspondence between the work and the man, the man and his environment. He went by the name of "le Père Corot;" Isnard calls him "le bon Papa Corot;" all his contemporaries speak of him with tenderest affection. Dumesnil says that in his younger years he was among the gayest of the gay at the dances held in the Academy of Design, and always wore a gorgeous yellow Spanish costume. Built like a Hercules, he was as jovial as he was robust. In his studio he wore a little cap

of striped cotton and a blue blouse. A
high, stiffly-starched standing collar and a
pipe were also part of his costume. To and
fro he went humming,

> " Je sais attacher les rubans,
> Je sais comment poussent les roses."

Charles Blanc says he was loved as a
comrade and respected as a master among
the landscapists, his juniors by twenty years.
"It is hard to say," he adds, "of how
many things his popularity consisted. His
uprightness and his good humor counted
for a good deal therein, his rustic air too,
his frank face, with fine and tender expression, and his joviality." William Hunt
says: "Corot was strong, stanch, decided,
cheerful about his own things. When I
saw him last he was seventy-seven. He
said: 'If the Lord lets me live two years
longer, I think I can paint something
beautiful.'" *

He painted smiling or singing. † While
at his work he was constantly exclaiming:
"Correggio, Giorgione, lend me your

---

* When some one remarked, " You, Corot, built as you are, you
will last one hundred years," he replied, "I—one hundred and four
years! I expect to obtain from the *bon Dieu les quatre au cent!*"
† Silvestre says: " He talks or listens to you hopping on one foot
or both." "When the public was all opposed to him, he said, with
his good and fine smile: 'They will come to it.'"

Corot at Work

brush!" He wandered about in a large blue
blouse, with great parasol, and was always
talking aloud with Nature, with the birds,
the butterflies, the trees. "Is it for me you
are singing, little bird? Well, this is fine!"
Every spring he fled to the country. He
said: "In the spring I have a rendezvous
with Nature, with the buds which begin to
burst, with the new foliage and with my
little birds, perching curiously on the end
of a branch to look at my work." He did
not like to have night come and stop his
painting, yet he would always remark
cheerily: "Well, I must stop, my heavenly
Father has put out my lamp." When his
day's work pleased him, he would say to
his mother: "A little fairy came, and, by
touching me with her wand, has given me
success."

He loved music passionately, but was no
reader. He had purchased a ticket once
for a symphony concert when Daubigny
happened in, and Corot insisted upon his
using the ticket. In referring to it afterward, he said that he had heard every bit
of the music in his room, shared Daubigny's
pleasure beside, and, "over and above all
that, here's Daubigny thanking me for it!"

He bought books on the Quays for their form and color, and put them in the hands of his models. He read, we are told, one book over and over again, selecting for that purpose Corneille's *Polyeuctes*. "For twenty years," one of his friends says, " he has been going over the first two hundred verses of this tragedy, but never gets to the end of it, and, when he talks of reading, he says: "But this year I must finish *Polyeuctes*."

His generosity was in harmony with the rest of his great, glad nature. He would never accept any money from his pupils and gave always generously, even when living on the modest income allowed him by his father. In 1855 he inherited an estate yielding annually 25,000 francs. Success in art came at about the same time, and he was soon earning large sums with his brush. He placed the inherited income out of his reach, allowing it to accumulate for his nephews and nieces, and the estate had nearly tripled at his death. His own habits were very simple, and he used the surplus of his earnings for his chief diversion, helpfulness to others.

He gave away many annuities, some, his

In the Forest

(From Nature)

In the Forest.
(From Nature.)

godson says, of 6,000 francs each. To encourage and assist his less fortunate comrades, he would pretend to be enthusiastic about their paintings and purchase them. The artist, Honoré Daumier, had become blind, and it was reported that his landlord was about to dispossess him. Corot purchased the villa and sent the title deeds to Daumier with the message: "This time I defy your proprietor to put you out of doors." Daumier replied: "You are the only man I esteem enough to be able to accept from him anything without blushing."

He made one year, near Arras, a study of a little peasant girl. On his return the following year he learned that the child had been drowned. Carrying his sketch to the father, he said: "Here is your daughter come back!" The peasant would never permit that sketch to be either loaned to an exposition or seen by any one but himself, and directed in his will that it be laid on his heart to sleep with him in the tomb.

Corot encouraged all who frequently sought his assistance to continue to come, declaring that it was a pleasure to him to help others. He said: "I would rather give to ten who are undeserving than deny a single one who is in want;" and again: "I never accumulate my revenues, and, from fear of a flood, I raise the gates every year; that is, if something remains over, I make a little distribution to all my nephews. . . . Those who are rich buy shawls for their wives, those who are poor buy mutton or petticoats."

Yet Corot never looked upon giving as meritorious; he had more than he needed and others lacked; he was simply readjusting the balance; besides, "it's nothing, it's my temperament and my happiness. I gain it back so quickly in painting a bough; that always produces for me more than it costs. I work better and with the heart more at ease. Once I gave away a thousand francs; that was all my pocket could stand for the moment. The next day I sold paintings for six thousand francs. You see that the thing had brought me good fortune, and it's always so."

When he foresaw, in 1870, that the siege of Paris was inevitable, he returned thither August 29th and remained until the end, helping those in need with his money, assisting in the ambulances, and

working hard all the time at his painting,
without which, he said : "I believe I should
have gone mad." When the national subscription for the liberation of the territory
was opened, he gave ten thousand francs,
and was deeply pained when it was returned to him because the plan had mis-
carried. And, most touching of all, it was
on his own deathbed that he learned of
Millet's death. Corot esteemed Millet
highly; but Sensier says they were never
friends, only acquaintances. Yet Corot at
once took measures to provide permanently
for Millet's destitute family.

Auguste Isnard says : "Of religion, Corot
loved only Christ and his teachings. He
had always in his room 'The Imitation of
Christ,' and it is in this favorite book that
he learned how to pass life in calm, and to
close his heart to the breath of ambition
and of egoism." What wonder that Burty
should say of him that he was perhaps
more loved than any other contemporary!

Corot's life, after his return from Rome,
resembles Millet's with those wide diver-
gences which the difference in their
natures and in their financial conditions
caused. Corot too had to struggle almost

until the end against the opposition of those in power in the art world. He was decorated after the Salon of 1846, and that persuaded his father to say: "I think I might allow Camille a little more money now."* But the battle continued still for a long time. Success came to him only at the age of sixty. After he had become famous, Corot said: "What an astonishing thing it is for me to find myself to-day an interesting man! What a pity that it was not told sooner to my father, who had such a grudge against my paintings and who did not find anything good therein because I did not sell them!"

The grand medal of honor was not given to Corot after the exposition of 1874. His friends had wished therefor, and considered it fitting as a final and full recognition of the master's work. A movement started in consequence among the artists, which led to a public subscription and the preparation of a gold medal, the gift of his friends and admirers.

Just at this time his sister, with whom he had shared the cottage in Ville-d'Avray, died. His own health, hitherto rugged,

* Will Low says that his allowance was doubled.

for he had never been sick, declined thereafter rapidly.

The dinner was given at the Grand Hotel
the 29th of December, three to four
hundred persons were present, and the dear
old master was welcomed with great enthusiasm and affection.

When the medal was presented Corot,
already sadly changed in appearance, whispered to the presiding officer: "One is very
happy to feel one's self loved like that."
It was the end; he went to his *atelier* at
times, but could not work, yet he loved to
linger there among his studies; he had
given scarce any away, and they were the
journal of his artist life. His pictures for
the Salon of 1875 were ready, lacking only
his signature, when his strength failed
him utterly. They were brought to him
as he lay on his dying bed; after signing
them he fell back, saying: "Behold all
that I can do." It was the last time that
he touched a brush.

A few days before his death he said to
Français, his favorite pupil: "See, I have
almost arrived at resignation, but it is not
easy, and I have been striving for it a long
time. Nevertheless, I have not to complain

of my lot; quite the contrary. I have had health during seventy-eight years, love of Nature, of painting and of work. My family consisted of brave folk. I have had good friends, and believe I have done ill to no one. My lot in life has been excellent, and, far from addressing any reproach to destiny, I can only thank her. I must go, I know it, and I do not wish to believe it; despite myself I conserve still a little hope, and (trying to smile) sometimes I would like to get near that soup I loved so well, and, if Madame T. put a good bit of cabbage in the dish, that would be perfect."*

On one of the last mornings he said: "I saw last night, in a dream, a landscape with a sky all rose. The clouds also were rose; it was delicious. I recall it very well. It will be admirable to paint." In his last moments he moved his right hand to the wall, his fingers seemed to be holding a brush, and he said: "Look, how beautiful it is! I have never seen such admirable landscapes." He died on Tuesday, the twenty-third of February, 1875, five weeks after the death of Millet.

Corot's methods of work were radically

* This was an allusion to the reunions with his artist friends.

The Bath of Diana

The Bath of Diana

different from Millet's. We know that all
of Millet's great canvases are the results of
deep experience, long and careful study,
and painfully slow and conscientious execution. Hunt says that he would work over
a canvas long after every one else thought it
finished, when the picture was sold and he
needed every franc that new work could
bring him.

Corot, we are told, worked rapidly, and
disliked to either spend a long time over a
canvas or to take it up anew, from fear of
dulling the spontaneity and the charm of
the immediate interpretation.

There is perhaps no word-artist, save
Shakespeare, whose natural endowment surpassed that of Lope de Vega. He heard
all the rhythmed voices wherein Nature
speaks; birds carolling, trees putting forth
green leaves, fountains sparkling, grain
fields waving, dashed with the scarlet
poppy; or where, in human life, as well
as in Nature, the strong, stern chords of
passion are struck. Singing as the birds
sing, producing without effort, he failed to
create a "Lear," a "Hamlet" or a "Pros-
pero." Yet how Nature shimmers through
Lope's verse! How perfectly he re-gives,

in poetic numbers, the tripping measures and the dewy atmosphere of the springtime!

Yet this is not said in criticism or in condemnation of Corot's methods. He knew best how to express what Nature said to him. That fresh grace, akin to Lope's, which he feared to tarnish by using the brush in hours when Nature was not with him, constitutes the distinctive charm of his canvases—to each artist, liberty and his own conscience as supreme judge!

Corot said: "To enter well into my landscapes one must have at least the patience to let the mist rise; one only penetrates therein little by little, and, when one is there, one ought to enjoy oneself." But we do not need to wait for the mist to rise in order to enjoy ourselves in that land of idyls, which is Nature and yet not Nature, a landscape seen in the real world, and then re-seen, transfigured, in the world of dreams. "I dream my picture," Corot said; "by and by I will paint my dream." We would not have Corot otherwise. We are willing to renounce the grand master rather than sacrifice the weaver of ballads.

Whose work is best done, his work is

highest; for to each of her interpreters Nature has assigned a special service, and who can tell through which portal of her many-doored temple the greater throng will come to find rest and renewal of courage. It may be at the proud portal of the drama, it may be at the humble gate of the ballad; it may be in an epic strophe of Millet, it may be in a summer idyl of Corot.

Théodore Rousseau

Rousseau

Barbizon

Rousseau's House at Barbizon

Rousseau

FOLLOWING the main street of Barbizon, some five minutes' walk beyond Millet's home, you will see on your left, through the bars of a broad iron gate, a charming little garden of flower beds and low trees. There is a tiny church to the right, in the rear of the garden. It is of recent date, having been built since the time of the great artists. Farther back to the left a nest of a house is hiding. Vines cover it completely; a stone stair leads, at the end nearest the church, to a loft which occupies the whole upper floor, and was once used for storing hay, but by Théodore Rousseau as an *atelier*. A photograph of Rousseau's time shows the vines peering in everywhere, scarce allowing space enough at the door for entrance, looking in at the bedroom window to wish good morning, and striving to clamber up the covered stair, leading to the master's *atelier*, in order to watch him at his work. The rooms are tiny, scarce large enough to contain the necessary furniture, and the rear garden is correspondingly small.

[131]

Man was for Millet the grand earth poem. But Rousseau said: "The tree which rustles and the heather which grows are for me the grand history, that which will not change. If I speak well their language, I shall have spoken well the language of all times."

Pierre-Étienne-Théodore Rousseau was born in Paris, April 15th, 1812, and was the only child of his parents. His father was a successful tailor, and a man of super-abounding kindness. He does not seem to have been able to resist any appeal for help, and his charities, with his indulgence toward his noble patrons, prevented him from ever accumulating a property. Sensier says that he gave away ten thousand francs at the time of the burning of Salins in 1825; Rouget de Lisle, the author of the "Marseillaise," was supported by him for years, as also a multitude of others, including political refugees of all nationalities, poets and vaudevillists. Rousseau's mother was a woman of superior character and charming appearance. The home was a happy one, the wife and mother its centre, and husband and son attached to her with a tender and respectful affection. A number of Rousseau's kinsfolk on his mother's side had already shown artistic talent. Her cousin, Alexandre Pau de Saint-Martin, was a landscape painter of some reputation. The boy, Théodore, loved to pass his free hours in the *atelier* of his uncle, as he called him, copying the paintings on the wall; but he always added something of his own, the wall itself, the nearest objects, in fine, all surroundings. It was a kind of instinct with him to give everything its natural environment. At the same time he was copying, with his pen, engravings, and displaying therein that same tenacity and patience of detail which characterized his mature work.*

When Rousseau was from twelve to fifteen years old he accompanied M. Maire, a friend and compatriot of his father, into the forests of the Franche-Comté. M. Maire and his brother had established a sawmill in a faubourg of Besançon for the

* Sensier records also the germination of another characteristic trait of Rousseau, his sympathy with the lower orders of Nature, his unwillingness to inflict suffering upon anything that had life. One day, while handling a lizard, its tail was broken off, and he would never thereafter touch one from fear of injuring it. As mature man, he preferred to bear with the ants and other insects that invaded his home rather than disturb them. Everything that lived, animal and vegetable, had for him its habits and its rights, and it was unjust and cruel for man to interfere. For the same reason he would never carry a firearm.

exploitation of the timber, and the lad served as aid and secretary. He saw now for the first time a forest in its wild state, and the trees charmed and intoxicated him. There he remained a year, when the failure of the enterprise caused him to return home.

It is supposed that his parents had chosen for him the career of civil engineer, but the lad took the matter into his own hands. He was the only child, and, while docile and affectionate, also resolute and persistent, and his parents stood loyally by him, always seconding every just desire. Providing himself with an artist's outfit, without informing any one of his purpose, young Théodore went one day to the Butte Montmartre, and, sitting down in front of the old church, "began to sketch whatever he saw before him—church, cemetery, trees, walls, and the upward slope of the land. In a few days he had finished a study which was accurate, firm and very natural in its tone."

The cousin-uncle, Pau de Saint-Martin, was consulted. He took the lad off with him to Compiègne, and had him make studies from Nature under his eye. On their return he advised Rousseau's parents to send him to Rémond, a landscapist, whom he esteemed as second only to Demarne among French masters. This occurred in 1826. Rousseau began therefore in earnest his art career at fourteen.

He was not pleased with the instruction received in Rémond's classical *atelier*. He always spoke of it afterward with contempt. "It took me several years to get rid of Rémond's spectres." He escaped, therefore, as often as he could from the *atelier régime* into the open freedom of Nature, making Sunday excursions to the charmingly wooded suburbs of Saint-Cloud and Sèvres, and, on longer holidays, pushing further out into the country. Once he traversed the Forest of Fontainebleau to Moret, some fifty miles from Paris, and made a study of the *route royale*. The natural school of landscapists had not yet come decisively forward; the classical school was in undisputed mastery. But Rousseau's instinctive aversion to the *atelier* rules and his intense love for Nature were already an indication of the coming revolt.

The Grand Prix de Rome, left vacant by Michallon's death, was open to competition, and Rémond desired to put Rousseau in training therefor. The pupil at first consented, and prepared himself to paint the classical trees and the proper heroic surroundings for the theme announced in the official programme; "Zenobia dead in the waves of Araxes, picked up by fishermen." But his artistic common sense revolted. "What need had they of digging up Zenobia in order to put soul into a landscape?" He gave up the task and played truant with more seriousness than before, sketching in the open air at Dampierre and the Vaux de Cernay, and in the dull winter days copying in the Louvre the animals of Du Jardin and Claude's landscapes. He studied the human figure in the *atelier* of Guillon-Lethière.

The year 1830 was an epoch-making one for Rousseau. He was then between eighteen and nineteen, an age when, if young manhood is strong, there is a joy in that strength and a confidence in its powers of achievement which seldom return with mature years. The spirit of the age, too, was youthful, revolutionary and Byronic. Rousseau had resolved to shake off entirely the academic fetters. Though his biographer does not state it in so many words, it is clear that he felt, if Nature alone were to be his teacher and guide henceforth, he must seek her out where she manifested herself in all her primitive strength.

He went therefore with a friend directly to the Cantal mountains in the Auvergnat, "a weirdly picturesque volcanic region," Mollett says, "where the hilltops spread in star-shaped ranges from a central dome, and between them are inaccessible ravines and noisy torrents rushing through with frequent tremendous cascades, and on the hills black forests of firs, alternating with wild scenery of barren upheavals of rock." Rousseau's eye became clear and his hand firm in the presence of this unshorn Nature, and his spirit, breaking entirely with the traditions of the schools, went forth in freedom and with ecstasy to gather in its first harvest.

Naturally the savage and bizarre aspects of Nature attracted him most. "He turned himself," Sensier says, "with a kind of delight to the most sinister mountains, the widest horizons, the secret places invaded by the capricious travails of the genesis. The country afforded him a vast uplifting of frightful precipices, where the Cère now plunges in impetuous rapids, now falls asleep in yawning abysses. He applied himself with insatiable pleasure to rendering a denuded rock, to painting the ruggedness of virgin soil, to sounding the giddy depths of black torrents and accursed whirlpools, as well as of gloomy caverns." This first season of freedom was one of revelling in Nature. He roamed everywhere about the forests and wilds, sharing with the goat-herds their bread and couch. He passed the nights frequently in the open air, watching the pallid light, seeking to know, to grasp, the life of that mysterious world of the night.

Millet went forth to the work appointed him as a mature man. He had counted the cost, a life-long struggle, poverty, and perhaps no recognition. Corot escaped to the summer land of his dreams; his servile years ended with the day when he went down to the bank of the Seine and began to sketch. Thenceforth his life flowed on as a river, calmly resolute, deeply peaceful. Rousseau made his choice in an ecstasy of glad communing with Nature, when manhood's strength leaped as an un-locked fountain within him.

Trees

(From a Drawing)

One stormy night he thought himself
lost in the vegetation of a morass without
limits. He was in water up to his arms
several times and in real danger. At day-
break he came to a pasture, upon a slope
of the ancient domains of Recoule and
Muret, and found there a goatherd in his
hut, who warmed him at his fire and
gave him a breakfast of buckwheat bread,
quail, and cheese made from goat's milk.
He remained there two days, running about
with his host and reconnoitering the whole
canton, and ended the adventure by dragging the mountaineer to the little city of
Thiézac in order to requite his hospitality
with a town feast.

On Rousseau's return to Paris with his
studies, his master, Rémond, "gave him
over to the infernal gods. His work, he
said, was the fruit of delirium, and there
was nothing wiser for him to do now than
to go back and live with the swineherds of
the Auvergnat." At this crucial moment,
happily for Rousseau, his parents had suffi-
cient affectionate confidence in him to
allow him entire liberty of action. Nor
was he long without an advocate, whose
judgment in artistic matters was respected.

Ary Scheffer was then known as a patriotic painter and a literary critic. The works of Rousseau were shown to him, and he was profoundly impressed. He felt that an original and robust talent was here marking out a path for itself. In his own youth and poverty he had received substantial aid and encouragement from Gérard, the official painter of the king, and it seemed to him the noble way of repaying that debt to aid in a similar manner a young artist of such unusual promise. He took Rousseau's paintings therefore, "hung them on the walls of his own *atelier* and called the attention of all his visitors to them as the works of a most original and incisive talent."

Rousseau had an immediate success. The young Romantic School saw in him an exponent of their ideas. The unconventional and robust spirit of his studies was in accord with the aspirations of that school, and with much of the earlier work of its master in literature—Victor Hugo. Here was an artist who did not hesitate to paint the rugged and bizarre aspects of Nature, without preoccupying himself as to whether such landscapes were in harmony with the traditions of the schools and the ruling laws of taste in art. It was enough for him that he had found them in Nature and had faithfully represented them, or interpreted what they said to him. Without seeking such distinction, simply because the march of his spirit was in harmony with that of the young generation, Rousseau became a champion of the new school. His work found also favor in the eyes of critics who were non-partisan, and all of them agreed that his studies marked a grand advance in French art in the direction of truth and naturalism.

Rousseau did not, in his elation over his success, remain idle and cease to advance. The recognition he had won stimulated him the rather to more earnest study. Though, in his work, a recognized leader of the young school, he took little part in the discussions of the day between Classicists and Romanticists. He preferred to think and work. He said later: "I thought only of one thing, to account to myself for the laws of light and perspective. I did not attach any importance to what they found original, new and romantic in *me*, I sought the picture."

During the day he worked in his *atelier*,

(9 Rue Taitbout), or in the open air at Saint-
Cloud, and took counsel of his former
master, Lethière, who advised him to study
in entire liberty. The evenings were spent
socially in the restaurants. A favorite
gathering place was at Lorentz's, 18 Rue
Notre-Dame des Victoires. Almost all the
members of that group have since become
known. They smoked a good deal but in
other respects, making a virtue of necessity,
were very abstemious. Water was their
regular beverage. Burette was able once to
offer five bottles of beer to the company,
numbering fifteen, and that evening was
marked with a red letter in their souvenirs.
Sensier says: "They talked about the
theatre, Hugo, Dumas, Barbier, painting,
actresses, the republic, travels; they made
charades, drew up programmes and established the Society of the Grelot (little bell),
which was nothing but a laboratory of
mystifications for the opponents of romanticism and a graft of the Society of the
Invisibles of Charlet. They picked the
Institute to pieces and laid an interdict
upon the Academy; the great volcano of
1830 had one of its little craters there."
Several times they appointed a rendezvous

at midnight at the Place de la Concorde in order to go from there without stopping to Dampierre or Chevreuse and return at once to Paris the next evening, a walk of fifteen leagues. Rousseau was one of the indefatigable; he made sketches *en route*, but talked little about his work.

In the following year, 1831, he exhibited for the first time in the Royal Salon of the Louvre. His picture was called " Site d'Auvergne," and was a souvenir of the bridge he had seen at Thiézac. It represented a valley bounded by the Cantal mountains. In the centre was a bridge with ruined arches. The public paid little attention to it, but the young school praised it. Jules Dupré, who afterward became Rousseau's bosom friend, had also four landscapes at the Salon and thus made his *début*. The peace and rustic charm which his work translated won for him immediately the public opinion, while Rousseau's bolder endeavors created both partisans and enemies and led to continual discussions.

Rousseau felt he must know more of Nature; he must see everything in order to understand and interpret. " He looked upon Auvergne," he said, "as only his first day of creation. There he had assimilated the spectacles of Titanic regions, of the commencements of the world and of the first sorrows of Nature; he had, in a sense, touched the age of iron and fire. He thought to make another step forward in studying countries that were in community of life with man, the rivers, the trees, the cultivated fields, the villages, and to attempt the exploration of the liquid element, the ocean, which gives to the phenomena of the skies their variety and their sudden movements." So a portion of 1831 and 1832 was given up to voyages of exploration into the unknown. He went first toward Rouen and studied the windings of the Seine, thence to Andelys where he sketched the Norman trees, the rocky slopes along the rivers, and the old castles; from there to Bayeux and the cliffs of Arromanches and explored the whole coast of la Manche and Calvados. He made a multitude of sketches and, in order to meet man under his native sky and know him too, he lodged in the country inns and mingled with the people.

The following year, 1832, he visited Normandy again, going directly to Mont Saint-Michel, and from this trip brought back the sketch for his Salon picture of 1833, "The Coast of Granville." This painting "placed Rousseau permanently in the front rank of French landscapists."* M. Lenormand, in writing the criticism of the Salon for that year, selected the work of six landscapists—Aligny, Cabat, Corot, Delaberge, Dupré and Rousseau for an especial examination. He said of Rousseau's painting: "The view of the coast of Granville is one of the truest things and the warmest in tone that the French school has ever produced. What M. Rousseau lacks is especially study . . . he is still far from his goal, but I would not give his future for the entire career of twenty of our most renowned landscapists."

Another round of the ladder was beneath young Rousseau's feet; this victory was a far more signal one than that of three years before, but he remained constant to his aim and unyielding in his demands upon himself. He shut himself up alone in his studio, and passed his days in meditation and his nights in painting. In the summer he returned to Saint-Cloud, but did not linger under the trees. He climbed to the

* Sensier.

heights, from which he could gain grand sweeping views, and there painted two panoramas—one from the terrace of Belle-Vue, showing the Basin of Paris and the course of the Seine, and the second from the terrace of Saint-Cloud, showing the valley of Meudon and the Isle Seguin. He made many studies here, and often returned from these days of communing with Nature too agitated to sleep, and passed the hot summer nights in his garret *atelier* in feverish intense work.

However rapid his achievement, his ambition far outran it. For the vision beautiful, more majestic, more alluring, with each larger, deeper insight into Nature with each day's work done, still eluded him. "I shall never grow old," he exclaimed once, "as long as I have my eyes to see." Had it been possible, Sensier suggests, he would have made of some aërial body a chariot, and, bending over it, have seized the grand forms of the earth, the river's silver in the entirety of its windings, the green and brown of the plains as a checkered whole, the forest as a single green bouquet. And, since that might not be, he would go to the mountains, for there

Nature appears in her grandest guise, thence
the outlook is freest. But he would prepare his mind through the lesser aspects of
Nature, although grand and primeval, in
order that the majestic beauty of the
mountain world might be read and interpreted aright. So he went down in November, 1833, to Chailly, on the edge of the
Forest of Fontainebleau, and took lodgings
with a peasant woman, *la mère* Lemoine.

Sensier says that the forest near Chailly
was then as virgin as in the time of the Mero-
vingians. The heather and oaks were its
lords, and the horror of solitude was there.
We have wandered about it recently: it is
still grand with trees centuries old, and huge
blocks of sandstone, tossed about in some
play of the giants. The heather still covers
with a robe of rose and misty green the open
places. But the wild beauty and strength
and the vast solitude of a primeval forest are
absent. Rousseau was too intoxicated to
work. That fever was upon him which
seized upon Millet and his friend Jacque,
when they first came to Barbizon.

He walked incessantly, and the night
found him often amidst the rocks, which,
in the moonlight, seemed huge, crouching

antediluvian monsters. "I heard," he told Sensier, "the voices of the trees; the surprises of their movements. Their varieties of form and even their peculiarity of attraction toward the light had suddenly revealed to me the language of the forest. All that world of flora lived as mutes, whose signs I divined, whose passions I discovered. I wished to converse with them and to be able to say to myself, through that other language, painting, that I had put my finger upon the secret of their grandeur."

In the evenings, in the peasant home, he was genial with all the world. Phrenology was a craze of the day, and Rousseau amused himself in searching out the aptitudes of the men about him, finding, as he wrote, "painters, poets, sculptors, diplomats, financiers, and verily even ministers in their natural state (*bourre*)." * "A peasant said to me: 'As for me, in the first place, I must command; I don't like to be opposed;' good for a minister. Another believes that the thunderbolt is an arrow that leaves the stars and comes to strike us, in order to talk a little roughly with us and excite us to answer; good for a poet."

* *Bourre*, literally coarse wool.

He remained in Chailly until February, 1834, and would have stayed the winter through, had not Ary Scheffer pressed him to return to Paris and deliver a painting he was preparing for the Salon, and had sold to the Duc d'Orleans before leaving for Fontainebleau. It was always a great sacrifice for Rousseau to part with a picture. He was never satisfied with his work, and forever retouching it. He brought back only a few studies from Fontainebleau, but expected soon to return there again with a mind calmed and ready to receive and interpret.

Meanwhile he made his preparations for a trip to Switzerland, intending to see everything, and not to return until the money received from the sale of his painting was exhausted. Just at this time he made the acquaintance of Jules Dupré, and the two young artists became at once the warmest friends. Dupré almost persuaded Rousseau to defer his trip to the Alps, making in its stead an expedition in his company "to the borders of the Bousane or the Vienne, into the country of swamps and high forests;" but Lorentz, a comrade from childhood, told him it might be the last time in his life that he could persuade himself he was a bird, soar above the mountains, share the society of the clouds and eat a bear steak. So Rousseau decided for Switzerland. A short time before starting, the director of the royal museums sent Rousseau an order for his Salon picture, which had already been sold to the Duc d'Orleans, and Rousseau could proudly reply that it was too late.

His star was ascending steadily and rapidly; admirers were multiplying and old acquaintances eager to claim him as friend. He was only twenty-two years old, and life, with all its splendid possibilities, ahead.

The friends, Rousseau and Lorentz, had taken a solemn oath to meet in Switzerland; Rousseau started first, and stopped *en route* at la Faucille, a mountain of the Jura range, with a wayside inn built of fir logs like the Swiss *chalets*. He planned to remain there a week while awaiting his comrade, but lingered four months. Mont Blanc had fascinated him, looking over from the distance across the lake of Geneva, and he had found at the inn a charming cavalier of the court of Louis Sixteenth, a nobleman with all the better qualities of

the ancient *régime,* liberal and progressive
besides. He loved Nature tenderly, was
brave and generous to a fault; Homer and
Horace were his constant pocket-com-
panions; with three score years and ten
well passed, he was as vigorous in mountain
tramps as a lad of twenty.

His relations, to prevent him from dis-
tributing his possessions among those in
need, had taken them away from him, and
reduced him to a meagre allowance. He
had in consequence taken refuge in the
mountains, where he could live without
control as Nature ordered, worshipping
God and loving his fellow-man in freedom.
Young Rousseau's fresh way of interpreting
Nature, his earnestness and enthusiasm, won
the old count's heart. He had been disappointed in his own son; he adopted
Rousseau in his stead, and called him *mon
fils,* and Rousseau repaid him with a like
affection. When the comrade (Lorentz)
arrived, gayety and the abandon of youth
took possession of the inn. The days were
given to mountain courses; in the evening
Lorentz sang Musset's odes; they danced in
the moonlight or talked philosophy, as the
mood suggested.

Rousseau paints himself to us in the confidences of a home letter to his mother.

"My good Mama:
  "I am always the same . . . always the same happy life, always fresh for seeing, vigorous for running, and diligent for one end. . . . The Mont Blanc is our alarm clock in the morning, our *vis-à-vis* are the folk on the other side of the lake of Geneva, (8 leagues). I could not say that we get along badly, though we do dispense with the ceremony of saluting each other and saying *bon jour* when we look out at the window, for we don't meddle in our neighbors' affairs. Our sight carries fifty leagues about us, and we are equally everywhere, although only occupying the space of our two feet. I am delighted with having received my stretchers in order to commence my view of the Alps. I burn with the desire of fulfilling the difficult task of giving upon canvas an idea of the immensity which surrounds me in order to distribute its benefits to those less fortunate than myself. . . . I ask without scruple, because it seems to me that I have something to give. I have so

much confidence in myself, *mon Dieu*, when I examine myself."

He had chosen as his great theme a picture of the Alps, and was busily studying Mont Blanc under all atmospheric conditions and at every hour of the day. Sensier describes a superb scene witnessed in September:

"The Alps had veiled themselves under an immense black cloud mass, which held all the sky and the earth; the thunder roared, and the lightning flashes suggested, behind that gloomy shroud, Mont Blanc always calm, always august, under the insults of the elements; when a horrible crash of thunder, such as Belshazzar must have heard on his last day, re-echoed in that vast conflagration of celestial wrath, and, after a few minutes of convulsions and struggles, the veil, rent and overcome, lifted and fled away; then the Alps appeared, virgins of light, radiant against a blue sky, blue as the dreams of paradise cannot imagine." The three friends, who had been silent for a long time, cried out with all their might: "*Vive Dieu, vive Dieu, vive le grand artiste!*" Rousseau painted,

as a souvenir of this scene, his canvas
—"View of the Chain of Mont Blanc
during a Tempest." He also made a study
of the inn after a night of snow and frost,
and this hung above his bed his life
through.

Rousseau's conduct had excited grave
suspicions. La Faucille is not far from the
Swiss frontier. A young fellow had been
seen prowling about in the most unseason-
able times and out-of-the-way places, always
noting down something and making sketches.
The sub-prefect of Gex, a French village
near by, thought the matter needed investi-
gation. So this worthy official, M. de
Montrond, presented himself at the inn to
examine the travellers and their baggage.
Lorentz treated him courteously, and, by
way of a flourish, turned a triple hand
spring, thereafter offering his arm as to a
grande dame, and escorting *Monsieur* to the
room where his comrade was madly at
work. Rousseau received his guest somewhat coldly, but invited him to be seated.
Unfortunately the one chair of the room
had vanished. A light dawned in the
worthy official's mind, and he proposed a
pipe for better understanding.

Some time later, as guests of M. de
Montrond, they witnessed from the balcony
of his official residence an imposing spectacle, the descent of the flocks from the
high mountain pastures at the approach of
winter. "A ruminant nation emerges
from the heights of the snowy peaks, and
spreads itself down the slopes to the lowest
pastures, resembling the precious stones of a
jewel box that a Polyphemus would throw
out of his cavern. The caravan descends
grave and slow, invades the ravines, winds
around the rocks, glides under the high
arches of the firs. . . . This migration,
of a Biblical majesty, continues for days
and nights; they hear it still in the
vagueness of the fog, and the horn of the
herdsmen, the lowing of the cows and the
tinkling of the bells, sound like the chords
of a pastoral symphony."

After visiting the Saint-Bernard, they
returned to Paris in December, 1834.
Rousseau had brought back a large number
of studies and at once set to work to prepare
a picture for the Salon. He chose for his
theme the "Descent of the Cattle." His
own *atelier* was too cramped for a canvas of
the size he wished to paint and Ary Scheffer

loaned him an *atelier*. The work was ready
in a few months and was offered to the
jury of the Salon of 1836.* They refused
it. Ary Scheffer, indignant, hung it on the
walls of his own *atelier* and invited all the
art world to come and see it. Jules Dupré
considered it an extraordinary creation.
Rousseau had, through inexperience, following Ary Scheffer's suggestions, used
pigments which have since almost destroyed
the painting. But, from the stir occasioned
by the action of the jury, from Sensier's
description, and from what we know of
Rousseau at the time, it is clear that, whatever may have been its immaturity, he had
put into it all the glory and the strength of
his artist springtime.

The jury of that period was an irresponsible body, its members holding office for
life. It consisted of the fourth class of the
Institute, composed of painters, sculptors,
architects, engravers and musicians. Rousseau, in some way, it would seem, either
through his social intimacy with a group of
young artists and writers of revolutionary
tendencies, or because of the prominence

---

*The Salon opened at that time in January, and works of art
intended for exhibition had to be sent in October or November of
the preceding year.

given to his work as the embodiment of a new school ideal, or for some deeper and unknown reason, had incurred the personal hostility of the ruling powers in the art world, and they had determined to crush him. He and his friends knew beforehand that no picture of his would be accepted at the Salon, and none was admitted until after the revolution of 1848 which did away with the old jury.

The year 1836 was thus a turning point in Rousseau's life. Since the state will command nothing of him, nor the Salon admit his pictures, those great creations whereof he had dreamed, must be given up for a time; for they demand large canvases—the Salon for their proper exhibition, and the state or a princely amateur as purchaser. So he turned from the mountains to the forest he had already learned to love, went down to Barbizon and established himself at Père Ganne's inn, lodging in a peasant's house near by.

The innkeepers of the artist towns of the forest, Barbizon, Marlotte, Grez, etc., divide their dining-room walls into wooden panels, and on these, as well as on cupboard doors and everything paintable, the artist guests exercise, in idle hours, their talents. Père Ganne's inn has disappeared, but its panels, and cupboard doors, have been transported to the garden of the new Hotel of the Artists, kept by his son-in-law at the entrance to the forest. There you will see more of Rousseau's work than of any other of the famous guests of that Barbizon hostlery, a charming panel of Corot, but nothing of Millet.

Rousseau met Aligny and Diaz at Barbizon. During the day he worked in the forest, especially in the gorges of Apremont. In the evening he traced in ink the series of sketches from Nature, which he was preparing as a study of the forest. Diaz was carried away by Rousseau's talent. When Rousseau started for a tramp in quest of a theme for his brush, Diaz followed, keeping always at a respectful distance. Where Rousseau set up his easel there Diaz might be found, a few paces away, painting a mossy rock or a tree trunk, but not venturing to speak. At last, one day, Diaz went forward and asked Rousseau to tell him the secret of his wizard coloring. Rousseau received him with open-heartedness, and that, says Sensier, was the point of departure of his (Diaz's) true talent.

"Speak of it to Diaz, whose beard has whitened with work and pain, and you will see his Castilian face light up, as at the souvenir of a great chieftain who led him to victory, and you will feel his heart expand at the memory of Rousseau."

The horizon was darkening in many quarters for Rousseau; his mother, passionately loved, died in 1837; the blow aimed at her son had struck her too; his father's financial position became embarrassed through his lavish generosity. The years that follow, until the revolution of 1848, are a season of severe discipline for Rousseau. It is doubtful whether he could have held himself strong, with undiminished creative force, had it not been for Jules Dupré. For he was, on the art side, supersensitive to criticism, pitiless in his self-demands, and merciless in his condemnation of work regarded, often morbidly, as imperfect.

He once said to Sensier, pointing to a painting,—"The Farm"—upon which he had worked for years: "Do you see that corner of canvas there, large as the hand, does it not seem to you that it far surpasses in intensity, in clearness, in expression, the rest of the canvas?" "Yes, without any doubt." "Well, then, all the rest must pass under the control of that little centre; all that which surrounds it submit itself to that diapason of light and the whole of the picture be as charged with life as that which you see there. Must we not incessantly lift ourselves, surpass ourselves, in this terrible profession of painter?" "But, Rousseau," objected Sensier, "with your reasoning, an artist would consume his life upon one picture." "What of that! Yes, a man ought to be courageous enough, loyal enough, and rich enough, not to produce but one prodigious work, in order that this work should be a *chef-d'oeuvre*, and glorify the man in his creation. And, furthermore, a great painter is only resplendent through a unique work. Michelangelo through his 'Last Judgment,' Rembrandt through his 'Night Guard,' Correggio through his 'Antiope,' Rubens through his 'Descent from the Cross,' Poussin through his 'Diogenes,' Géricault through his 'Medusa;' all that they create thereafter are always the children of giants, but inferior to their elders. If I could have my wish, I would be a millionaire for nothing else save to effect the genesis of a single and unique picture, to consecrate myself thereto and to find my pleasure therein, to suffer and joy in it, until, content with my work, after years of trial, I could sign it and say: 'There my powers stop and there my heart ceases to beat;' the rest of my life would be passed in making designs, in painting for my relaxation, studies which would be only flowers thrown upon the work whereof I would be content."

Seeing him absorbed at the end of a day, Sensier asked: "Well, Rousseau, are you content with your day?" "Ah, my dear friend," he answered, "never is a day long enough, never is night short enough; have you ever thought of that vain fellow, that impudent *monsieur*, who is called Pygmalion, so satisfied with his own work that he fell in love with it? I should like to know that presumption. It must be a crushing happiness, but I shall never attain thereto."

Sensier tells how Dupré saved at least one canvas, "Border of the Forest," which Rousseau, morbidly critical, was about to injure by overpainting, or destroy altogether, by urging him to turn it face to the wall and give it a long month's lease of life. When the month had expired, he examined it long and searchingly in Dupré's presence, finally exclaiming: "Well, I am going to sign it; it is finished."

On the human side, Rousseau's nature was rich indeed in its social capacities and powers of enjoyment. Pierre Millet, brother of François, says: "One could not be near Rousseau and not love him." Yet, as seen in the biography of his friend, Sensier, he was one who peculiarly needed companionship.

Both of an age, Rousseau and Dupré became as brothers in their friendship. Whatever may have been Rousseau's counter gift, we know that Dupré gave to him cheerfulness and courage, and was, for all the time of their comradeship, a helpful balance wheel in his troubled existence. To unite in a close alliance the artists, whom the jury had put under its ban, Dupré gave frugal fortnightly dinners, at which Ary Scheffer, Decamps, Eugène Delacroix, Barye, Chenavart and Rousseau were present. Ary Scheffer, though not among the outcasts, was generously the most outspoken in his criticism.

The brother artists were weary of the Paris world and eager to live somewhere together, where they needed but to cross the threshold to find Nature and could forget all about Salons. So in 1841 they went to the native country of Dupré's parents, to a little village Monsoult, on the borders of the forest of Isle-Adam. Their studios were door to door, Madame Dupré, Jules's mother, presided over the home, and the days interlinked themselves as the lines in an idyl. In 1843, in Paris, they had studios side by side; neither ever went out for an evening without the other and no invitation was accepted that did not include both.

In the following year, they went south to explore the barren heaths of Gascony, of whose picturesqueness alluring reports had come to them. After passing Bordeaux and Mont-de-Marsan, " they visited those strange sandy countries, where the aborigines take care of their flocks, mounted upon stilts, where for leagues and hours one only sees dunes and sand plains, only vegetation, which is neither grass nor lichen, seeking to cover the ground with its clutching creepers. . . . They descended to Peyrehorade (Pierre who rolls), a charming little city, which seemed to them a specimen of those happy nooks where one lives upon the blue of heaven and the murmur of the water; from there to Tartas, thence to Begars—a happy country of woods and warmth; everything pushes forth there with the vigor of the tropics, melons climb the trees, lemons and orange trees grow as robust and fresh as our apples, in company with oaks as majestic as those of Fontainebleau. The dwellings of rough wood and thatch are built under the shadow of the oaks and even in their branches. Man there loves the tree, which protects him from the wind and sand. . . . Finally, close to the forest, through the maritime pines, appears the Gulf of Gascony, the wave blue as a sapphire which, without wrath and without obstacle, arrives, calm and strong, from the shores of America."

There Rousseau began work on two paintings, " The Farm " and " The Village Bakery," which, with a third, " The Village," were to occupy him the rest of his life, and there the friends struggled in vain five months with the constant fathomless blue of the southern sky. " What man touches, he can become master of," Dupré said, " but to paint that sky without clouds,

The Farm—Sketch.

that well of light, is as hopeless a task as it would be to sound its depths." They gave it up at last, put their knapsacks on their backs and visited on foot a part of the Pyrenees, traversing the Basque country; but they had sworn, " by the oaks of Begars and by the blue ocean, to meet every spring at Whitsuntide on the square of the village of Begars, in order again to start forth for the discovery of the azure, the blue without limit, in its immaterial essence."

But the times became harder. Rousseau had often, between 1837 and 1840, revisited Barbizon and lingered there on into the winter, after all others had left. He allowed himself therefore to be persuaded now, under the tranquil charm of the forest, that it was not well for man to see more than once in his life such agitating spectacles as the Basque country and the Pyrenees offered. One of his favorite forest haunts was Belle-croix, a region of rocks, heather and low trees, overlooking the valley of the Solle. A few twisted, dwarfed trunks stand there to-day, the decrepit survivors perhaps of a weird, gnarled forest of Rousseau's time. Rousseau said to Sensier, " Ah, silence is golden; when I was at my observatory of Bellecroix, I did not dare to move, for the silence opened to me the course of discoveries. The family of the forest then bestirred itself. It is the silence which has permitted me, immovable as I was as a tree trunk, to see the stag in his lair and at his toilet, to observe the habits of the field rat, of the otter and the lizard, those fantastic amphibii. He who lives in the silence becomes the centre of a world; for a moment I would have been able to believe myself the sun of a little creation, if my study had not recalled to me that I had so much difficulty in aping on my canvas a poor tree or a tuft of heather."

Rousseau loved the trees as individuals. For him each had a distinct character, and temperament and he would fain know each one apart. Thus he could come close to the heart of that great community we call the forest and, after years perhaps, his brush would be able to interpret to man the thought and sentiment that live within trunk and branches and disclose themselves in the outreaching of arms to the sun, in every movement, in every silence.

In September, 1867, two months before

A Sketch

A Sketch

his death, when already half paralyzed, he took a ride with Sensier to look once more at the heather. "Pointing to the Sully, a giant of the wood, he said: 'One winter's day I saw it covered with snow, white as a warrior of Ossian. It extended its arms like an old bard, a branch fell at my feet and might have killed me. It would have been a beautiful death, there in the heart of the forest, killed by an oak and perhaps forgotten upon the heath for years. Do you see all those beautiful trees there? I sketched them all thirty years ago; I have had all their portraits. Look at that beech there, the sun lights it up and makes of it a marble column, a column that has muscles, limbs, hands and a fair skin, white and pallid, as that of the Hamadryads. . . . See the modest green of the heath and its plants, rosy, amaranthine, which distil honey for the bees and fragrance for the butterflies. The sun lights them up and gives them a diapason of extraordinary color. Ah, the sun, it is the Lyre of Orpheus, it makes everything move, feel, attract, it makes the stones eloquent!'" When on his dying couch, he said: "I watch for the ray, which traverses the poplars and comes to me. It brings me still the good odor of the leaves and the cry of the insects. I have still to learn and to profit."

Rousseau's long absences from Paris only aggravated the situation produced by the hostile attitude of the jury.* Dupré, who was always the elder brother in their councils, decided therefore that they must show themselves in Paris and make a brave appearance to attract buyers. So they hired, at 2 Place Pigalle, two fine studios, with each a suite of rooms attached, on the first floor of a building constructed for painters. The young militant school gathered there and it was there also that Sensier made Rousseau's intimate acquaintance.

Rousseau's finances were, at this time, very straitened. Sensier says he had scarcely money enough "to keep him in tobacco." His art-outlook too was dark. No amateurs came near him, art dealers scarce ventured to hang his paintings in their windows. The Salon condemnation had borne its fruit. Dupré exhibited two of his comrade's canvases in his own *atelier* and, after infinite discussion, disposed of both for six

* In 1845–6 he was again for a long time at Isle-Adam with Dupré.

hundred francs. Sensier, writing in 1871, says that 42,000 francs had been offered for them. The friends made Millet's acquaintance, but their poverty seemed luxury to poor Millet, and he drew back into his isolation.

The following year, 1847, Rousseau became engaged to one whom he loved deeply, who was worthy of him and returned his love. The engagement was broken. Sensier will not lift the veil. May we read between the lines, Rousseau's poverty, dark future and sensitive pride? He fled to the Forest of Fontainebleau, walking incessantly, that in fatigue he might lull sorrow to sleep. He hired from a Barbizon peasant, for a brief season, a tiny thatched cottage at the end of his garden, two rooms and a loft, and remained there the rest of his life.

The revolution of 1848 created a short-lived republic. One of the first acts of the new government was to satisfy the artists. A painter, M. Jeanron, was named director of the Museum, and in lieu of the old Salon and its irresponsible jury, it was resolved to accept everything offered and to allow the entire body of artists to elect a commission for hanging and awards. Rousseau did not exhibit, but both Dupré and himself were named members of the commission. Ledru-Rollin, the Minister of the Interior, at the suggestion of the new director of the Museum and of Charles Blanc, director of the Beaux Arts, went in person to the studios of Rousseau and Dupré and ordered of each a canvas at four thousand francs, a sum then regarded as enormous. This act was intended as a public reparation to the artists who had been persecuted by the old *régime*.

It would be natural to expect that the unlucky star which had dominated Rousseau's firmament for twelve years would set now and fortune make amends by unusual graciousness. But this was not to be. How much his lack of balance, how much the survival of the old hostility to him, as an innovator in art matters, or as one affiliated with Thoré and other political radicals, contributed to this result, it is impossible for us to determine.

In 1849 Dupré, who had not exhibited, received the Cross of the Legion of Honor. Rousseau's three pictures were badly hung and he was awarded only a first medal.

Forest of Fontainebleau—Setting Sun

He said: "The simplest field-flower would suit my button-hole better, but I feel myself wronged; I am not understood." This difference in awards led to an estrangement between the two friends, the fault being, so far as we can discover, wholly on Rousseau's side. Two years later he had a somewhat similar experience, Diaz being decorated and he remaining without recompense. Diaz conducted himself in royal fashion. At the official dinner of the artists who had received the decoration he rose and, in the presence of the heads of the Administration, proposed the toast, "To Théodore Rousseau, our forgotten master."

The following year, 1852, brought an official reparation. Rousseau had resolved not to exhibit and the time for sending in canvases was past. The Director of the Museums came to his studio in person and pleaded with him to be allowed to take some of his canvases and hang them on the walls of the Salon. Rousseau yielded and was at last decorated with the Cross of the Legion of Honor. This gave him a standing before the public and was the beginning of a brief period of fame and abundance.

Sensier describes Rousseau in his prime,

"He was of middle stature, very vigorous and made for walking; his head was olympian and strikingly resembled Shakespeare's, his eye kind and fine, his look that of one who fears nothing because there is nothing to fear, his hair black and curly, his forehead proud in its tranquillity and strength."

His conception of the relation of Art and Nature is well expressed in his reply to Guizot. The Duc de Broglie had ordered of Rousseau a painting of the Château de Broglie, intending it as a souvenir for his friend and colleague in the Ministry, M. Guizot. Madame Guizot had died there, and Guizot urged Rousseau to make the painting grave and sad, and, as far as possible, an interpreter of his own feelings. Rousseau replied:

"If my painting depicts faithfully and without over-refinement the simple and true character of the place you have frequented, if I succeed . . . in giving its own life to that world of vegetation, then you will hear the trees moaning under the winter wind, the birds that call their young and cry after their dispersion; you will feel the old château tremble; it will tell you

that, as the wife you loved, it too
will . . . disappear and be reborn in multi-
ple forms.   If, in fine, I have thrown upon
my canvas the mighty breath of the creation, which engenders to destroy, I shall
have interpreted your thought. . . . Our art
is only capable of attaining the pathetic
you wish to refind in it by the sincerity
of its portraiture. . . . One does not copy
with mathematical precision what one
sees, but one feels and interprets a real
world, all of whose fatalities hold you fast
bound."

Rousseau desired to be a millionaire, in
order to devote his entire life to one painting.   An opportunity, akin to this, was
provided for him by Frédéric Hartmann,
who ordered and paid for three paintings,*
allowing Rousseau all the time he wished
for their execution.   He was busied upon
them during fifteen years.   Death alone
put an end to the travail and permitted the
purchaser to claim his canvases.

Sensier says, "They passed through
phases, now marvellous, now lamentable.
Millet and I were the only ones permitted
to catch a glimpse of them.   Indeed, at

* "The Farm," "The Village Bakery" and "The Village."

times, he hid himself from us, when the work assumed sombre tones and vigorous accents. Then there took place on his canvases a kind of aërial tragedy, which disheartened us. The silhouettes of the trees became menacing, the forms of vegetation shrivelled, the features of the landscape became petrified in a dull despair. Rousseau seemed to be chastising his work . . . in return for his long labor of creation, by condemning it to the most lugubrious and painful metamorphoses. Then on other days we saw them reborn, as limpid, joyous and scintillating as the mornings of springtime." . . . " ' The Village ' was one of his torments. The day before it was sent to the Salon even he worked upon it with a fury that disheartened us. In a single day, trebly-locked in his studio, he transformed the entire sky. He had thrown himself with abandon into Japanese art and, dominated by those beautiful oriental auroras, which unite so well, in just balance, the softness of dawn and the ardor of the tropics, he had made for that poor hamlet of Picardy, a firmament where Buddha would have chosen his throne of light. . . . Later he refashioned it again and turned back to

[174]

our melancholy horizons, to our skies sad and gray.*

M. Castagnary said of Rousseau: "He does not carry us away, as François Millet, toward the sorrowing epochs of rustic life, to reveal their savage grandeur or gloomy solemnity . . . he does not transport us as Corot, into the lands of twilight, where the light, the freshness and the shadow sing an aërial melody, whose last notes reach out into infinity. No: simple, strong, all impregnated with naturalism, he respects the exact relations of the trees, the animals, man and the sky."

Before turning the last pages in the journal of Rousseau's artist career, we must visit him in Barbizon in the home which, from 1848 on, another shared with him. A young girl, of humble parentage and poor, came to him in Paris in 1848, seeking his protection. He sheltered her and she became his wife. The relation between them was a most affectionate one. She was not his companion in the higher life, and his friends appear to have looked upon her as a kind of chattering magpie and a burden on

* "The Hoar-Frost," a culminating point in his art, was, on the contrary, finished in eight days.

account of her ill health, yet it is plain that, to Rousseau, she was a tenderly loved and most tenderly cherished child-wife. Her chatter was refreshing song to him, whatever it may have been to his friends.

Sensier is almost impatient with Rousseau for that father and lover spirit, which the strong man showed toward this weak singer of Béranger's chansons, who had found her way into his home; but he recognizes the complete blending at the last of their existences. He went to visit them during their honeymoon in Saint Martin's in summer. "The little house was covered with clematis, nasturtiums and cobeas. One felt the presence of a woman in that coquetry of hermitage." Rousseau had found his happiness and his old inspiration. He spent all his time in the forest and made charming studies there. One of these, "The Little Hillock of Jean de Paris," contains a picture of his wife. The autumn wind is moving in the birch trees. A young woman, in a blue dress, is sitting at work at the foot of a tree.

Rousseau's letters to his wife are in charming contrast with his usual epistolary style. He who is always serious, restrained, in contrast to Millet, stiff and cold almost, becomes free, glad and merry to joviality. His letters for the first time sing; not a grand epic strain as Millet's, or a ballad of nature as Corot's, but a light chanson, such as those his wife was wont to repeat.

"Thou must get good round cheeks, for otherwise I shall use them all up for thee at once. . . . I think of thee every moment, savoring beforehand all the pleasures I shall have in leaving the train, from seeing thy dear face calling me with thine eyes. It's idle to say that the absent are at fault; it is not true when one loves them from the bottom of one's heart. See, thou art becoming apotheosized for me, thou gainest every day, thou hast never had a fault, thou hast never tormented me, not even on theatre days. . . . Thou art, in fine, such that I only need thy presence to be happy all the days of my life. . . . *Au revoir*, my darling little one . . . I embrace thee as I love thee. My father, Millet, Sensier, Daumier, embrace thee; the whole family, *le bon Dieu, et le Diable*, embrace thee. . . . P. S. As for the pheasant, I hear a gun-shot, that must be the Père Baudouin,* who is making

* A neighbor who had promised Rousseau a pheasant for his wife.

his first essay. Patience, patience then, and enjoy a foretaste of it. Latest News: The pheasant is still living, but they talk about bringing a stuffed one from Paris. . . ."

The fat years had begun for Rousseau. His thatched roof was changed for one of tiles, he bought rare bits of old faience from the peasants and picked up etchings of Rembrandt, Ostade and Claude Lorrain. " At this time the home of Rousseau was a little hospitable centre, full of attentions and charms; the friend arrived there without other announcement than his presence. Rousseau received him with that smile and that child's glance which signified, ' I expected you.' We talked painting, Paris, literature, we hailed Millet, who was working, still unknown but courageous in his country *atelier*, we passed comments upon the masters, the setting sun, the light and the longevity of man. The months were years, to-day they are only days."

A culminating point came with the Universal Exposition of 1855. Rousseau exhibited thirteen paintings and won a decisive victory, due however rather to the appreciation of Americans than to that of his own countrymen. Millet had sent but one canvas, "The Grafter." Rousseau was enthusiastic about it. One day Sensier was amazed to learn from Rousseau that he had sold Millet's canvas to an American for four thousand francs. Sensier was beside himself to discover who this extraordinary individual was who was willing to pay four thousand francs for a canvas which would not have brought one thousand in Paris or in all Europe. "But consider," he said, "Rousseau, that astonishing man has been enlightened, as St. Paul on his road to Damascus. What a rare organization that of a being, new and without education, who arrives from his deserts and feels himself all at once drawn toward an expression so simple! Don't you see, we need not despair of anything?" "Ah, well! my friend, to-morrow he will come to see me, come, don't fail." "The next day I arrived at the house and, extending his hand, Rousseau said in a low voice: 'Well, here he is, he is here. Yes, it is I, since you will know it. But swear to me that you will say nothing about it. I want Millet to believe in the American, that will encourage him and that will make us both more free, for I wish to purchase other pictures from him.'" Those were glad days in the vine-covered cottage. Rousseau, delighted by his unexpected good fortune, loved to gather his comrades about his long poplar table in the loft *atelier* under the tile roof. "Diaz excited the hearty laughter of Rousseau by his caprices, as unexpected as the humorous explosions of Goya; Daumier was in the mood of Rabelais; Barye sparkled with sarcasm and biting tales about pedants and prudhommes; Millet thought no more of his wretchedness and talked about his Norman country and his family souvenirs."

But with 1857 the clouds gathered again. The Salons were not favorable, unfriendly criticism became keen once more, apparently not altogether without reason, for, to judge from Sensier's account, Rousseau was painting rather mechanically and work that would sell. His biographer tells also a strange story of the venomous pursuit of a Belgian picture dealer, who bought up Rousseau's pictures at a high price and then auctioned them off at a low one so as to make Rousseau's rating low!

Fortune did not smile on Rousseau again until 1865. During these years he was compelled to sell at auction his little collection of bric-à-brac, was burdened with debt and constrained on that account to re-visit Paris every month, for a time every fortnight, so as to be at his legal domicile to meet his creditors. His wife's health failed from nervous weakness—she was pass-ing into hysteria.

In 1863 he had made a second visit to la Faucille, thirty years after the first. As before, he sat facing Mont Blanc. What memories of old ambitions and youthful dreams must have returned! The rain fell upon him in torrents, but he would not move. An inflammation of the lungs re-sulted therefrom, which was almost fatal and from which he seems to have never en-tirely rallied. His friends became anxious about him and plotted for his relief. One of them assumed, as he supposed, all his debts, but unfortunately Rousseau had not made a full confession. A retreat was pro-vided for his wife and the day of her re-moval set. But, at the moment of de-parture, Rousseau withdrew his consent. "Ah, my dear friend," he said to Sensier, "when I think that I shall dry up the source of so many treasures of tenderness, in separating myself from her, from her who is but a spoiled child, I feel that I am very unjust to procure my repose at the expense of her heart." He remained steadfast in his refusal to the last hour of his life.

Rousseau's fortunes, ill and good, had all his life through much of the unexpected about them. So it was in 1865. The Count, Paul Demidoff, ordered two wall panels of Rousseau at ten thousand francs each. Similar orders had been given to Corot, Dupré and Fromentin. While Rousseau was at work upon this commission two young picture dealers offered him one hundred thousand francs for sixty canvases, all the old studies of his youth, and forty thousand francs additional for other work unfinished. In 1866 he was invited to the Emperor's court at Compiègne, and in 1867, at the Universal Exposition, was elected President of the International Jury, received one of the eight grand medals of honor,* sold paintings for two hundred thousand francs and gratified his love for the works of the old masters to the extent of buying thirty thousand francs' worth of engravings at one sale. Three Expositions were opened

* Four for France—Cabanel, Gérôme, Meissonier, Rousseau. Four for other countries—Kaulbach, Knaus, Leys, Ussi.

Landscape with Animals

simultaneously, the Universal, that of the annual Salon, and a third at the *Cercle des Arts*. Rousseau was represented by a hundred and twenty-four works. His triumph was grand and complete. Hostile criticism was silenced.

But that same malevolent influence that had dogged his steps hitherto dropped into his brimming cup that which made its every drop bitter. His comrades of the jury and his fellow medallists were all made officers of the Legion of Honor, he, the President of the Jury, was excepted.* It was the *coup de grâce;* the tension had been too great since 1836; paralysis came upon him, he lingered, moved dying about his garden, followed by his hysterical wife. Millet was constant in his devotion. The end came December 22nd, 1867, "the grand harmony" following upon the tragedy of his life.†

* His French comrades of the Jury were Gérôme, Pils, Français and Corot. He was made Officer of the Legion of Honor before his death.

† Two days before his death he said, expecting to recover: "There will be a crisis and thereafter the grand harmony will come."

Antoine Louis Barye

Barye

Barye's House at Barbizon

Barye's House at Barbizon.

Barye

ANTOINE LOUIS BARYE was born in
Paris September 15th, 1796. His father
was a goldsmith. His family preserved as
souvenirs of his earliest childhood figures of
animals that he had cut out of paper, and
said that he used to mix pounded brick
with water and paint therewith designs
upon the wall. He was not sent to any
lycée, but at thirteen apprenticed to Fourrier,
an engraver in metals. Fourrier was charged
with furnishing the metallic portions of
the military equipments, the helmets, gor-
gets, eagles and crosses of honor. The
repoussé work for the gold snuff-boxes which
Napoleon I. was in the habit of presenting to
his brother sovereigns was also executed there.
Young Barye was employed in the preparation of the molds and dies for all classes of
work, from the buttons of the uniforms to
the finest products of the goldsmith's art.

The conscription of 1812 took him at
sixteen away from the workshop, but fortunately his training for his later career was
not thereby altogether interrupted. He
was attached at first to the topographical

brigade of the engineering corps and soon
after incorporated in a battalion of sappers.
He told Sylvestre that he "worked night
and day on reliefs of Mont Cenis, Cherbourg and Coblentz, which are probably
still preserved in the archives of the War
Department." March 30th, 1814, as he
was returning wearied from a long walk
across the fields of Montrouge, the porter
of the military depot called out to him
through the wicket: "The army has left;
go with all speed to rejoin it on the banks
of the Loire." Montrouge is at the gates
of Paris. Barye was penniless and thus un-
able to follow the army in its retreat. So
he returned to his father's house.

The capitulation of Paris freed him from
military service, and he resumed his work
as engraver, but he said: "I was tormented
by my vocation for statuary. I applied
myself with infinite zeal to drawing and
modeling, but, as I was not one to stir
about, I neither knew how to find a master
nor how to arrange matters so as to live as
student." He solved the problem by making his handicraft supply the wherewithal
for his studies and entered in December,
1816, the studio of Bosio. Bosio was a

conventional worker of the old school, without originality or strength. The equestrian statue of Louis XIV. of the Place des Victoires, and the four-horse chariot of the Arc du Carrousel, show his incapacity for monumental work. He was not, however, without a certain fine feeling in his treatment of the nude, as the "Hyacinthe" of the Louvre Galleries shows. Barye had come to his studio in order to learn the rudiments of the sculptor's art, and to this extent only is he probably Bosio's debtor.

Three months later, in March, 1817, he entered the studio of the painter Gros, and apparently for a time frequented both studios. Gros was a pupil of David, and the author of several large canvases now in the Louvre. Barye's biographers agree in attributing to Gros more influence over him than Bosio exercised. Gros was an enthusiast, full of energy and a strong worker. Arsène Alexandre says of him: " Classicist by conviction, the first of the romanticists by temperament, he exercised the same influence over all the great painters who went forth from his hands. They observed what he did and listened as little as possible to what he said."

Guillaume says: "Barye appeared in the midst of a passion of renewal which began to seize upon the French school. The study of history and the knowledge of foreign literatures were enlarging the field of inspiration. With several artists this romanticism was signalled by a return to nature and science. Géricault may be considered an example. His anatomical designs have remained celebrated. He modelled. While painting the shipwreck of the Méduse he surrounded himself often with corpses." The 2nd of July, 1816, the Méduse was wrecked forty leagues off the western coast of Africa. A hundred and forty-nine persons took refuge upon a raft. Twelve days later the brig Argus rescued the survivors, fifteen in number, when at the point of death; the rest had been claimed by the sea, or devoured by their companions. Géricault represents the raft at the moment when the brig heaves in sight. It is covered with livid, distorted figures, dead and dying. The canvas, exhibited in 1819 when Barye was twenty-three, made an epoch. Géricault's work is considered to have exercised a sensible influence upon Barye.

In the year 1819 Barye presented him-

self for the first time in a *concours* for
medals at the École des Beaux Arts. The
subject was a medallion, " Milo of Crotona
Devoured by a Lion." He received the
third prize. Opinions differ with regard to
the merit of this first published work of
Barye ; some, as Gustave Planche, discover-
ing therein the promise of all his future
powers, others seeing no such revelation.
The question is of slight importance.
Barye's schooling is far from finished yet ;
his creative career, in the monumental
sense, still distant. The following year,
1820, he entered the competition for sculpture, winning the second prize. The theme
was " Cain Cursed by God after the Death
of Abel." For four successive years he continued to compete, but unsuccessfully. In
1823 no prize was awarded, the exhibits
being considered below the grade demanded.
In 1824 Barye's work was not even
admitted.

Already, since the preceding year, Barye
had been in the employ of the goldsmith,
Fauconnier, of the Rue du Bac, and he now
abandoned the Beaux Arts entirely and returned to his craft. Fauconnier was pur-
veyor by appointment to the Duchesse de

Berry.*   Here Barye remained eight years, or until 1831, and here it was that, under his own direction, he gained his art education.   He was married at the time and two daughters were born to him.   Beyond this, and that wife and daughters died, that he married again and had in his second marriage a family of eight children, we know almost nothing of Barye's private life. He was by nature and resolution taciturn, and his life, in contradistinction to that of his brother artists of Barbizon, has for us only the art side.   But that is so grand in its steel-like tenacity of purpose, so splendid in its steadfast growth, that we need no opening of the home doors in order to know and be inspired by the man Barye.

While Barye was still at the Beaux Arts, he studied the Egyptian sculpture which Champollion was arranging in the Louvre. He learned much therefrom and more probably from the Assyrian sculptures, discovered and brought to France a score of years later.   To the Greco-Roman collections of the Louvre he was also, and in a large degree, debtor.   But Barye gathered information, as the trees absorb the ele-

* The Duc de Berry was the second son of Charles X.

ments essential to their growth and fruit bearing.

Nothing was neglected by him during these years of discipline that could contribute to the development of his talent. He had no theories to advance in the wars of the schools; he was not militant, not even a talker, but he had determined where and how to pursue his studies. Though no biographer quotes a sententious declaration of his dating from this period to the effect that Nature is the first and last teacher to be consulted by one who would represent life, such was clearly his resolute, quiet decision as to himself and his studies henceforth. He drew from the human model in Suisse's *atelier*, he familiarized himself in the amphitheatre, and through dissection with the physical structure of men and animals; he informed himself thoroughly about the best methods of melting and casting metals; he made himself an expert in every branch of his craft; he copied in the Louvre the works of the masters.

The Jardin des Plantes was, however, his great studio, not merely at this time, but thenceforward throughout his life. Many changes in the line of growth and expansion

have come doubtless since Barye first began
his assiduous visits there seventy years ago,
but the general features are the same. The
Jardin des Plantes is not merely a menagerie and herbarium, but contains also a series
of museums illustrating all the different de-
partments of natural history, with library,
laboratories and lecture rooms, wherein to
work over scientifically the material col-
lected, and train students in the branches
of knowledge there represented. In the
Garden the different animals are to be seen
living, moving behind the bars of their
cages; in the Museum of Zoology you will
find them stuffed; in the Museum of Comparative Anatomy, founded by Georges
Cuvier, you can study their skeletons as
connected wholes, all the bones of their
structures separately and, in many cases,
casts, representing their bodies in various
stages of dissection. This was the day of
the Cuviers. Frédéric, the younger of the
two brothers, had been named curator of
the menagerie in 1804.

Barye made constant use of every facility
of instruction afforded by the Garden, the
Museums of Natural History, the Menagerie
and the galleries of Comparative Anatomy.

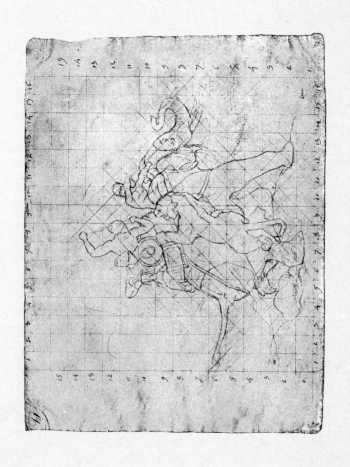

A Study—Barye

A Study—Barye

He studied Buffon, Cuvier, and works
upon history and mythology. It is clear
that he had already in mind the representation in statuary of heroic and mytho-
logical incidents. He attended the courses
of lectures. When an animal died he was
at once notified by a messenger from the
garden and, dropping everything in hand,
hastened thither. He measured, drew and
sometimes modelled the animal before or
after dissection.

The Père Rousseau, who was the keeper
of the ferocious animals, had become his
especial friend. "He opened to him at
five o'clock every morning the doors of
the menagerie and, when he saw him draw
from his pocket a few poor crusts of hard
bread, he handed to him some fine slices
of tender bread taken from the daily
rations of the bears." Père Rousseau lived
long enough to see his protégé become
famous, and he loved to talk to the young
artists who visited the Garden about the indefatigable ardor "of that thin and tall
young man, always silent, who first found
the beasts of Père Rousseau worthy of being
reproduced." He it was who sent a messenger to notify Barye whenever an animal

died. The two glories of his life were "that he had formed Barye and that he had conducted the Emperor Alexander in 1815 about the menagerie."

In sum, Barye, having seen others preferred to himself and his own work con-demned at the Beaux Arts, resolved to equip himself for the career to which ambition and a steadfast will held him, by acquiring a comprehensive and accurate knowledge of the higher organized beings, living and dead, and at the same time to train eye and hand in the workshop until he had become a master in every detail of his craft, the practical working of the metals. Furthermore, the great artists of old must yield to him the secrets of their power and inspire him to work, which would earn for him also the rank of master.

His work for Fauconnier passed of course under the master's name. We know that he was asked to make a stag for a soup tureen and, after studies in the Jardin des Plantes, executed the order. The clients were not satisfied, it was "too much like nature, not noble enough." The official report of the Exposition in 1825 states: "We owe to M. Fauconnier a collection of

The Tiger and Crocodile

The Tiger and Crocodile

good models for the imitation of divers animals." It is not unfair to the master to find therein a recognition of his employé's work.

After four years spent in such studies Barye made his first Salon exhibit in 1827. The true beginning of his creative career did not come, however, until 1831, when he was thirty-five. He made then exhibits both in painting and sculpture. Two of the three works in sculpture attracted general attention, a "Martyrdom of St - Sébastien" and a "Tiger Devouring a Crocodile." The last, which was one-half life size, was the corner-stone of Barye's reputation and of his artistic career. The criticism of the day shows the surprise and enthusiasm which the work created. Charles Blanc says that "the young (romantic) school was astonished and delighted by the accent of truth, liberty and the sentiment of life therein. For centuries ferocious animals had only been treated conventionally. The idea of studying them at the menagerie had never occurred to anyone." The academic school, then in entire control, despite its prejudices, was constrained to recognize him and awarded him a medal of the second class. He received also an order for a bust of Louis Philippe.

The St-Sébastien model, given into the charge of the administration of the Louvre (Barye having no suitable place for it), has disappeared, broken doubtless and carried away bit by bit, but the "Tiger" was cast in bronze and in 1848 purchased by the state. It is to-day in the Louvre galleries. The chief interest of this group is from the comparative side. It shows the point of departure of Barye's creative life. It is strong, as all of his work, but it lacks the grandeur and the poise of his masterpieces. The posture is one of tense repose. The great cat is crouched upon all fours. The tentacles of his muscular fore-paws hold the victim as in a vice. He is looking down upon the writhing amphibian. In another moment he will crunch the life out of his feeble prey and gorge himself with the dark blood and the palpitating flesh. The crocodile is an image of weakness in the fast clutch of pitiless strength.

And yet the sculptor has not attained the freedom and breadth of his maturity. The hairs even are indicated. The body does not slip forward with that tense and tre-

mendous muscularity, that feline ductility,
which the living tiger of the Jardin des
Plantes, surlily pacing back and forth in his
narrow cage, and Barye's jaguar of 1851,
show. Had Barye created only this tiger
and the other masterpieces, which represent
this stage in his development, he would
scarcely have won a secure immortality.
He had broken a path, pointed out a
new field, astonished and surpassed his
age; yet the calm breadth of execution, the
majesty and dignity of immortal works,
of his own later creations, are lacking. But
Barye never rested, never slackened his
efforts to assure and broaden the foundations
of his art through the study of nature and
of the masters, to give suppleness to his
hand, exactness to his eye, by constant exercise and observation. His talent shall soar
upward, but on strong, even pinions; knowledge shall balance and guide enthusiasm.
His life from 1831 forward is therefore as
the slow, steadfast ascension of a star.

Charles Blanc says that the life of an
artist when Barye's career began was not
what it is to-day. The world sought them,
not they the world. Their social life was
passed in the artist reunions at the cafés and

restaurants. Such a gathering-place of artists and men of letters had been established at the Barrière du Maine at the Mère Saguet-Bourdon's. Barye and Sainte-Beuve were among the first admitted to this circle. The artist Charlet and Alexandre Dumas were also among the comrades. Béranger came sometimes. Here the grand battle for the triumph of Victor Hugo in Hernani was prepared.*

There was no Salon in 1832, the cholera preventing it, but in 1833 Barye exhibited six water colors representing animals, a frame containing medallions, a bust of the Duke of Orleans, and ten other works of sculpture, the most notable of which was the "Lion and Serpent." Barye had left the shop of Fauconnier in 1831 and begun his independent career. All his leisure since the exposition of the "Tiger" in that year had been spent in the Jardin des Plantes. This exposition showed the results.

The effect produced by the "Lion and Serpent" was greater even than that caused by the "Tiger." The celebrated critic, Gustave Planche, who appreciated from the

---

* The first representation of Hernani, the 21st of February, 1830, provoked in the parterre a veritable conflict between the Classicists and Romanticists.

outset Barye's powers and gave him in his criticisms helpful counsels, says: "The 'Lion' created a general cry of astonishment among the partisans of academic sculpture. Very soon the astonishment gave place to anger, for the public, despite the remonstrances which the professors and all who swore by their maxims addressed to it, obstinately persisted in praising Barye as an artist as happy as he was skilful." Barye was decorated with the Legion of Honor; the "Lion" was purchased by the State and placed in the Garden of the Tuileries. The group is there to-day. It shows an advance upon the "Tiger" of 1831, yet it belongs to the same epoch in his development.

We have styled the lion the king of the beasts. Looking upon him as personifying in a supreme degree the nobility and strength of the brute creation, we have made of this king of the wilds an impersonation of that brute force which alone is worthy to serve the highest types of manhood or humanity in those employs which are the most heroic. We have harnessed him to our chariots of victory, we have placed him as guard at the portals of our temples and palaces, we have installed him

as watch by the tombs of our heroes, we
have made him the prop of the thrones of
our kings.   But the lion, as a grand, splendid, savage life, finding its beginning and end
in self, we had not studied, scarce con-
ceived, until Barye came.

The type of the conventional lion is
a familiar one.   His body is limp, without
bone, muscle or nerve; his face elongated, venerable, stupid; his eye dull, opaque;
his mane falls in long, heavy curls, strikingly resembling, as Théophile Gautier
suggests, the wigs of Louis XIV.'s time;
his paw rests upon a ball.   He could not
harm, to roar were impossible.   It is
doubtful whether the granite has not in its
pores blood enough for that torpid existence.   With this image fresh in our minds
—a pair of these nondescripts face the Place
de la Concorde, one at either side of the
Tuileries Garden—let us go and stand
before Barye's group.   The kinship is ap-
parent in the elongated face, in the form
and in details, but Nature is shaking off
conventionality.   What savagery in that expression, what truth in that attitude!   How
marvelous that relaxed right paw, whose
keen claws have cut through the serpent's

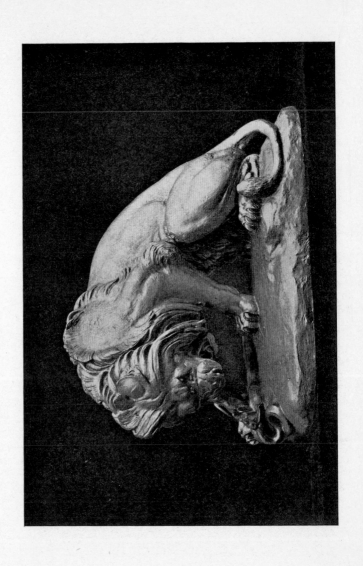

The Lion and Serpent

The Lion and Serpent

coil, relaxed that in another instant the
clutch may be fast, mortal! How sugges-
tive of the loathing of the nobler brute, of
his involuntary shrinking from the fanged
serpent, that head lowered and turned aside!
That lion lives and, if you wait long
enough, you will hear the deep growl of
the wilds escape its opened jaws. And yet
it is, though nobler, of the family of the
tiger of 1831. There is the same care in
details, the same lack of breadth, grandeur,
calm strength.

Gustave Planche said: "I shall reproach
M. Barye with suffocating the life of his
animals under a multitude of details too
pettily reproduced. Less literally exact,
the sculpture of M. Barye would be grander,
more beautiful; it would be less real, but
more true; it would gain in elevation what
it would lose in puerile fidelity." Alfred
de Musset wrote, when the group had
been cast in bronze in 1836: "The
bronze lion of M. Barye is as terrifying as
Nature. What vigor and what truth! . . .
Where indeed has he found a way of making such models pose? Is his *atelier* a desert
of Africa or a forest of Hindustan?"
Charles Lenormant said: "The more I saw

that combat of the lion and the serpent, the more the impression grew; it seemed to me at first the lion moved, yesterday I heard it roar."

Théophile Gautier declares that the old conventional lions scattered about the public gardens almost let go of the balls, "which keep them in countenance," when they saw Barye's lion. When the State had purchased the group and placed it in the Tuileries Garden, one of the academicians exclaimed: "Since when were the Tuileries a menagerie?"

Despite the opposition which the novelty of Barye's work and its success with the public had provoked in the academic camp, the promise of the future was rich indeed. He was but thirty-seven. The academic jury even, as we have seen, had been compelled to recognize him. The royal family were his patrons. Roger Ballu, in his biography, gives an engraving of him as he appeared at this time and accompanies it with a word painting: "The head slightly bent, the eyes large, dreamy, intelligent, lively, not flashing, but wide open and reflecting a certain melancholy, give to the face the expression of a man who examines, observes,

meditates, scrutinizes, then resolves, and has
the energy of his decision." We read in
the face strength, a mind alert, questioning,
almost suspicious.

The Duc d'Orléans, Louis Philippe's eldest son, ordered of him a massive table-
piece, in gold and silver, which was at first
intended to be of reasonable dimensions and
wholly the work of Barye. But M. Aimé
Chenavard succeeded in intruding his per-
sonality through Barye, in his good-nature
and his desire to be helpful, permitting his
own work to be surrounded by a certain
amount of architectural work of this artist.
The final result was that M. Chenavard assumed the direction of the whole. If it
had been completed according to his designs, it would have weighed nine thousand
kilogrammes. When the first piece of the
structure was brought, it was discovered
that the table would not support it. This
was a trivial thing. M. Chenavard ordered
forthwith a new oak table of the proper
solidity. Unfortunately he had not taken
the measures of the dining-room. When
the table was placed therein, no space was
left for the chairs. Another triviality for a
man of M. Chenavard's devices! He pro-

posed to push back the walls of the Tuileries, but the architect, out of patience with
this jesting, interfered, and M. Chenavard,
disappointed in his dream of adding perhaps a new wonder to the seven, died
broken-hearted. Though M. Chenavard
had a successor, the table-piece was never
finished. Barye's work would have embraced nine groups. He was busy upon
them for many years. They were not
ready in 1848, the year of the Revolution
which expelled Louis Philippe and his family from France. In 1863, they were sold
in fragments at the sale of the property of
the widowed Duchesse d'Orléans. The
five principal groups represent five grand
hunts, of the tiger, the bull, the lion, the
elk and the bear; the four minor groups,
combats of animals.

The years that followed until 1837 were
busy and prosperous ones for Barye. He
was at work upon the order of the Duc d'-
Orléans; the Duc de Nemours, Louis Philippe's second son, the Duc d'Orléans as
well, and the Duc de Luynes were among
the purchasers of his bronzes. Only a few
new works were exhibited at the Salons, as
his strength was given almost entirely to

the execution of the table-piece. There
was question at this time of charging Barye
with the execution of a monumental work
of supreme grandeur. Thiers was minister
from 1832 to 1836, and eager to commem-
orate in stone, in some surpassing way, the
Napoleonic glories. He seems to have had
a great diversity of ideas as to the method,
and to have been carelessly generous with
promises to artists, which were not fulfilled.
The matter is unclear; but we know that
during these years the most inspiring pros-
pects were held out to Barye; now it was
the decoration of the entire Place de la Concorde, now of the four corners of the bridge.
The plan which assumed the most definite
form, was that of crowning the Arc de
Triomphe with some grand work in statuary.
Which of the two, Barye or Thiers, first
suggested the imperial eagle is uncertain.
Charles Blanc says it was Barye's idea. The
plan, if carried out, would have given an
eagle, with seventy feet span of wings, de-
scending upon the arch, and while still half
supported by the air clutching in its talons
trophies symbolizing the cities and nations
curbed or crushed by the genius of Napoleon.

[207]

Nothing came of all this, but in 1835 the State asked of him a Sainte-Clotilde for the Madeleine. The story goes that Barye wished to chisel a saint bearing his wife's name, but this grace was not given him. This opens for an instant the fast closed door of that home and shows us that love reigned there. The Madeleine figure, strong, pure, noble, is not unworthy of Barye, but as one looks from the Place de la Concorde up that sloping way of the Champs-Elysées, unique in the world, and sees the triumphal arch at the end, standing forth symmetrical, beautiful against the sky, one can but regret that France did not give to him, as Athens to her great sons, work worthy of his genius.

The jury of thirty-six, that struck Rousseau and limited his talent and thus the glory that France would have won therefrom, had spared Barye. But he did not look for a continuance of such consideration from men who had closed the doors of the Salon to Delacroix and Rousseau. He was not therefore disposed to exhibit as yet the parts of the table-piece, several of which were ready. But the Duke of Orleans insisted, saying, "I will take charge of it."

The bronzes were refused. The duke, indignant, asked the king to interfere, but Louis Philippe answered: "What do you wish? I have created a jury, I cannot force it to accept *chefs-d'oeuvre*." Jules Dupré, meeting Barye, asked him how his work prospered. "It is going very well; I am refused," answered Barye. Dupré was indignant. "It is altogether natural," said Barye, "I have too many friends on the jury."

This action of the jury, when compared with that of the preceding year, seems to indicate the purpose of serving a sharp notice upon the young school that the old canons of art could not be violated with impunity, and the approval of the public did not carry with it the commendation of experts in art matters. The reasons alleged, that the groups of the table-piece did not belong to the domain of sculpture but to industrial art, and that they were, furthermore, *genre* works, seem rather props to support a weak cause. Barye interpreted the action in the sense of an order to submit, or cease to compete, and withdrew altogether from the Salon until the old jury had been swept away with the monarchy. He did not exhibit again until 1851.

The year 1837 marks thus in Barye's life, as the preceding year had in Rousseau's, an epoch. As Rousseau turned from his earlier limitless ambition, to be the interpreter of Nature in her grandest manifestations, to the trees of the forest of Fontainebleau and was content to express their speech in "that other language, painting;" so Barye turned largely away from monumental art, in the grand sense, to the creation in bronze of those charming little animals, which were called by his contemporaries, half in pity, half in scorn, paper-weights.

The royal family continued to support him. The Duc de Nemours and the Duc de Luynes desired also to have table-pieces from Barye's hand. The Duc de Montpensier, fifth son of Louis Philippe, ordered a chimney-piece. Only one of these works, the last, was executed, and the principal group, intended to be placed above the clock and representing "Angelica delivered by Roger," a theme from the Orlando Furioso, is greatly admired.

During the years prior to 1840, he received and executed a commission to furnish certain portions of the Bastille column. The lion that is walking about the base of

the column, and the cocks at each of the
four corners of the pedestal, are Barye's
work. The Bastille was captured by the
Parisians and torn down July 14th, 1789.

The lion is the zodiacal sign of the
month of July. This "Lion of the Bastille"
is another mile-stone in the onward march
of the great sculptor. The details that
weaken the lion of 1833 have disappeared : the head is nobler ; the artist is
working with greater freedom and breadth;
one step more and he will attain the majesty
of the highest art. The lion is pacing with
slow measured steps about the base of the
pillar erected in memory of the brave,
breathing low growls as he goes. Charles
Blanc says of this lion: "It is the image
of the people guarding their dead."

Barye the artist answered the action of the
Jury of 1837 by making himself a manufac-
turer, hiring skilled workmen, watching
strenuously over every detail of the fabrica-
tion of his art bronzes and selling them himself. These bronzes embrace not merely a
Lilliputian menagerie, and a series of statu-
ettes, but also candelabras, perfume burners,
fenders, candlesticks, cups, even inkstands.
Shall we regret or rejoice that the great

artist was constrained to make his art sub-
serve the needs of the multitude? Despite
all our admiration for these Lilliputians and
our personal satisfaction that a cat or rabbit,
a lion or tiger, may serve us as a paper-weight,
when we stand before one of Barye's sublime
creations, we do regret the worse than folly
of French art rulers from 1837 forward.
There stood an artist, such as the centuries
yearn for, clear-headed, firm-handed, approaching the zenith of his power. He
would have done for Paris in the interpretation of animal life, and of animal and
human life combined also, what the masters
of Greek art did for Athens.

These lions and tigers, bears, deer, horses
and dogs; these eagles, storks and pheasants,
crocodiles, serpents and turtles; these flying,
walking and creeping, wild and tame crea-
tures from Lilliput are grand despite their
diminutiveness. The modeling is always
that of a master. Because they were little
things of base price, they were not therefore despicable in his eyes. He signed
them. He signed his candlesticks and inkstands also. Go to his workshop, he is a
master who knows better than his best
workmen—for he has the broad compara-

tive standpoint—every detail of the man-
ufacture. Every product must satisfy
him; if imperfect, it must be melted over;
if his hand is needed in some mechanical
detail, he puts on the green apron and
shows his employés how the work should
be done.

From the financial side, the venture was
not a success; he supposed naively that the
merit of his work would draw the public
to him, but it did not. With a large dependent family, carrying a heavy debt* and
harassed by creditors, forced, in order to
satisfy them, to give them his models as se-
curity, and knowing that inferior casts were
being made from them and the models in-
jured, not a free man in definite possession
of his own until 1857, Barye walked forward unshaken. His work, his art, suffered
not an iota. With Olympian calm he
worked and awaited the justice of the slow,
sure years. Arsène Alexandre says: "His
friends never heard him utter complaints or
cry out against the rigor or the folly of the
age."

Nor was the grand art, the monumental,
altogether neglected. The "Theseus and

* Incurred in order to establish a foundry.

the Minotaur," though still rather statuette than statue,* is already Greek in its serenity, and belongs to the Grand Art. With 1847 he sent forth from his *atelier* the "Sitting Lion." That was his first public answer in monumental work to the closing of the Salon doors. The answer was a complete one. It is the lion, the king, who is sitting there. We doubt if ever brute majesty has been as perfectly represented. Here all pettiness, all small lines, are effaced. Terrible in his conscious might, ord of the brute creation, he sits there as on his throne, looking forth to the ends of the world, and there is no life, winged or four-footed, that does not bow before the lion, the king. The State purchased it to make amends, it is said, for his failure to receive the commission to decorate the Arc de Triomphe, and placed it in the Garden of the Tuileries not far from the "Lion and Serpent." It was removed later, and now faces the Seine at one of the entrances to the Louvre. A pendant was desired, and Barye prepared a model (since cast), but his price was too high. A replica was made at the State's order by purely mechanical processes,

* Original dimensions 47 centimetres in height by 31 in length.

The Sitting Lion

the head turning to the right instead of the left. Barye was indignant, but had no redress.

M. Fremiet visited him in his studio in 1846 when he had begun work on the "Lion." "All the lines were fixed. The preparation was anatomical. All the important bones of the skeleton were in place, each separately added, the skull, the vertebral column, the cage of the ribs, the bones of the anterior and posterior members. . . ."

In a souvenir of artist gatherings, quoted by Dumesnil in his biography of Corot, we find Barye and Corot charmingly associated. "The thirteenth day of the month, which was in Rome that of the grand Ides of April, he (Corot) took part with our comrades in the dedication of the ancient head of Jupiter Philios, protector of friendship . . . . the father of the profound and ingenious Minerva, of the laughing Venus, of Apollo and the adorable Muses, the tolerant God, venerated by Pythagoras and Phidias, as much as by Homer and Orpheus. An eloquent invocation was pronounced by one of the great-grandchildren of those who reared temples to him, and, meanwhile, two torches were held before the venerable image, the one borne by M. Barye, the other by Corot."

Arsène Alexandre describes a dinner which united regularly Barye, Corot, and a number of their fellow artists. "They had the habit of defiling before a big (*un grand diable de*) Jupiter of the Vatican, whom all, united in the same antipathies, loaded with all the imprecations intended for the Institute." One of the events of every such gathering, awaited with curiosity, was Barye's turn. "*Ha!*" Corot would cry gaily, "*il a été très digne.*"

Forty-eight came, and with it the revolution. By it Barye lost and gained. His royal patrons were driven out of France, but the Salon doors were no longer closed to him. Of the commission of eleven, chosen by the artists to have charge of the sculptures of the Salon of that year, Rude was chosen first, Barye third. This was the day when the outstanding accounts of aggrieved artists were balanced in part. Barye, as Rousseau and Dupré, received orders from Ledru-Rollin, the all-powerful leader of the Republican party, now Minister of the Interior. At the suggestion of Charles Blanc, Director of the Beaux Arts,

Barye's "Tiger" of 1831 was purchased by the State, and Ledru-Rollin, furthermore, named him Conservator of the Gallery of Plaster Casts and Director of the Louvre Studio of Moulding. Until Barye's time, the position had been considered a business opportunity. The Louvre studios furnished duplicate casts for the European galleries. The moulds, purchased by the director, served as long as they would hold together. How the interests of art and of public instruction fared under such a *régime* may be imagined. Barye changed all this, put the best casts on turning-tables, made a choice of statues for reproduction, ordered new moulds, and surrounded himself with a corps of skilled workmen.

Barye re-entered the Salon of 1850 with two works which represent the full maturity of his powers. The "Centaur and Lapith," afterward called "Theseus Combating the Centaur Biénor," and the "Jaguar and Hare." Both are in the Louvre. Théophile Gautier said: "That Centaur, overcome by a Lapith, shows that Romanticist, proscribed by the Jury, to have been the modern sculptor who approached nearest to Phidias. . . . . That Lapith of robust and simple forms, beautiful as the ideal, true as nature, could have figured in the pediment of the Parthenon . . . . and that Centaur have joined the cavalcades of the metopes."

There are in the Louvre galleries to-day two bronze casts of antique sculpture—the originals are in the museum of the Capitol in Rome—representing centaurs, beside a marble group, "A Centaur Conquered by the Genius of Bacchus." The three are almost identical in pose and in their main lines. There is a conventional model of the centaur, and these three statues are slightly varying copies of one original. The hind legs are near together, the right fore-leg raised and bent backward. In the marble, the head also is curved backward, and the hands joined behind to express the subjection of the half-brute to the child Bacchus, who bestrides it. One of the bronzes has a similar *motif*. The hands of the centaur are, however, bound instead of being clasped, and there is no child upon its back. There is a certain rude strength and a suggestion of a life of the woods about these antique sculptures, but of motion, of intense living in any form, there is slight trace.

Cross the Louvre court and enter the

The Centaur and Lapith

The Centaur and Lapith

room where three of Barye's masterpieces
have been placed side by side. The "Tiger"
of 1831 and the two exhibits of 1851. It
is clear, from the striking analogies in pose
and lines, that the "Centaur and Lapith" of
Barye come after the antiques, but the half-
brute of Barye is not their descendant.
The lines and moulding are all stronger,
nobler. The hind legs are placed far apart,
the right far forward. That creature was
an instant since running as the wind, and
the forward impulsion of the whole body is
tremendous, despite that violent arrest which
has bent backwards the right hind pastern.
That half-brute has its stall in the woods,
on the free crags, and the storm wind is its
playmate. The tail stands up a splendid
shock of bristling hairs. You can read the
whole story there: immense, shapely brute
strength and suppleness, with every muscle
tense to bursting, and yet the spirit cowering.
The Centaur knows that a master bestrides
it. And Theseus!—he is one of the Olym-
pians, serene, severe. His raised hand will
strike but one blow, and that will crush as
the thunderbolt.*

* Both the Theseus groups were retouched during many years.
Sometimes he left a model ten years before casting it.

And now leave the Louvre, and taking one of the little Seine steamers, a swallow or fly (*hirondelle* or *mouche*), as you choose, visit the Jardin des Plantes, and stand before the cages where the great cats are confined, the lions, the Bengal tiger. Notice the grand savagery in the face, the packed muscularity of every part, the slip of the whole with every movement. What elasticity, backed by what projectile power! It is as elusive as the sunset hues in the clouds, as the dance of light upon the forest carpet. What sculptor can seize that? Return to Barye's room in the Louvre and look at the "Jaguar devouring a Hare." If you put your hand upon the bronze, you will feel the slip of the muscles beneath the tense skin. Barye has missed nothing, neither the spring nor the strength. His jaguar is life, and the life of the forests, which is other than that of the cage, and is not an individual but a type. That is the new element which he has discovered and added, the immortal soul he has breathed into the bronze. And that is genius.

We do not care to follow Barye the sculptor farther, step by step. He has attained immortal things already. He will

The Jaguar and Hare

The Jaguar and Hare

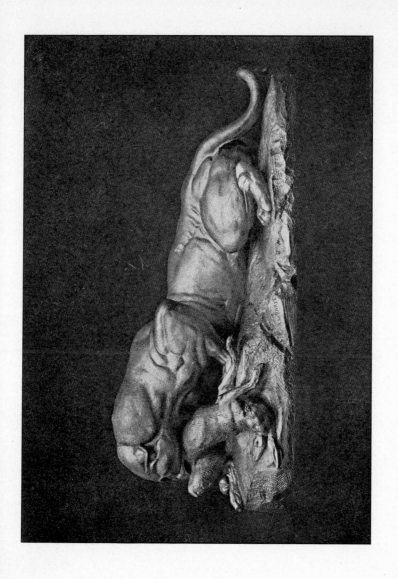

not advance. Not that advance were impossible for him, but his years and strength are now in their full maturity.

Barye had just finished a pendant to the "Centaur and Lapith" in the Louvre one day in 1850, when he received word to withdraw at once. The order to vacate was so sudden that Barye could think of no better way of removing his new model to his home on the other side of the Seine at the Montagne Sainte-Geneviève, than to hire a hand-cart. He followed it, picking up the fragments of the clay, as they were broken off and thrown out by the jolting over the cobbles, and when the house was reached, there was nothing but fragments. He was named, we are told, as a sort of apology, professor of drawing at the agricultural school in Versailles, but the position was suppressed the following year. It meant nothing and probably was so treated by Barye.

The "Jaguar" appeared in bronze at the Salon of 1852 and was purchased by the imperial house. The fourteenth of October, 1854, Barye was named Professor of Drawing in Zoölogy at the Museum of Natural History at a salary of two thousand francs a year, raised in 1863 to two thousand five hundred francs. He held this position until his death. He was also charged with the decoration of the pavilions, Denon and Richelieu, of the new Louvre. The chair at the Jardin des Plantes must have been a great gratification to him. There where he had come, untaught by the schools and refused at the Beaux Arts, to study directly from Nature when but an artisan, he came again thirty years later, recognized as a master in animal drawing. We are told that his teaching limited itself to such remarks as these: "Look at Nature and make your choice;" "What shall one teach in presence of that (Nature)?" He was apt to forget himself *en route* and would be found standing before one of the cages.

The action of the Jury of 1837 had sent Barye back to the workshop. We are tempted to think that, with that deep, silent determination which was the basis of his character, he resolved then and there, as a producer of these same little things, scorned at the time as of the jeweler's craft and *genre* works, to win at some future day complete brilliant recognition. It came with the World's Exposition of 1855. He was member of the Juries of admission and of awards; he exhibited in the Section of Beaux Arts the "Jaguar" only, but placed in the Section of Industry a collection of his models. The International Jury unanimously awarded him the grand medal of honor in the Section of Art Bronzes, and he was thereafter named Officer of the Legion of Honor. When the Central Union of Beaux Arts applied to Industry was founded in 1863 he was named president, and in 1868 he was elected to the Academy of Beaux Arts.

The public work of Barye's last period embraced the four groups for the two pavilions of the new Louvre; the decoration of the pediment of the pavilion of the Horloge; the equestrian statues of Napoleon I. for Ajaccio (Corsica), and a similar statue of Napoleon III. for the Porte du Carrousel—this last was torn down in 1870—also groups in stone for Marseilles. The most important of all are the groups in stone for the pavilions of Denon and Richelieu. They represent War, Peace, Strength protecting Labor, and Order punishing the Perverse.

[223]

The constituents are the same in every group, an animal (horse, bull, lion, tiger) reclines in the background, a man and a child occupy the foreground. These groups recall in their serenity and grand lines the "Theseus" of the Louvre galleries, and reveal a kinship with Greek sculpture.* Barye does not seem himself to have been entirely satisfied, or he felt that his powers were waning. He said one day on the scaffolding before one of these groups, " They give me to eat when I have no more teeth," and similarly, later, referring to the Statue of Napoleon III., " I have waited all my life for customers and they come at the moment when I am closing the shutters."

One of the most perfect of all Barye's single figures of animals is the " Lion walking." It was cast in silver and given by the Emperor to the winner of the *Grand Prix* of 1865. There was great excitement at the time. To the delight of all good Frenchmen, the English horse was beaten and a Frenchman won the hundred thousand francs and the Emperor's gift. This lion is now in the possession of Mr. Walters, of Baltimore.

* Guillaume considers the human figures here greater than in the two groups of " Theseus."

War

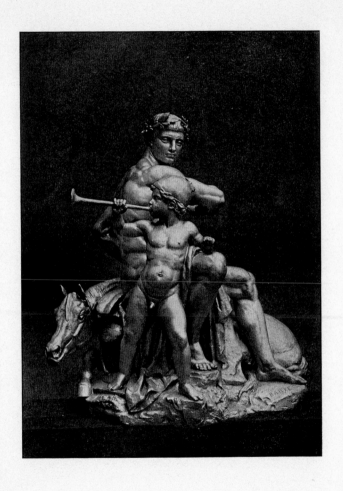

Sylvestre, Barye's friend, describes him as
he knew him at the zenith of his powers
and reputation. "He is of supple figure
and above middle height; his dress is modest and careful, his bearing and gestures are
precise, tranquil, worthy; there is nothing
dry or pedantic about him. His eyes vigi-
lant, firm, look you always frankly, profoundly, in the face without provocation or
insolence. The brow is losing its short and
iron-gray hair; the nose is slightly turned
up; the parts of the face, of a vigorous
squareness, are finely connected."

"Barye looks at you, waits for you, listens
to you with patience, and divines infallibly
your thought. All his words hit the mark,
but they seem to come forth with effort from
his thin, strong lips, which are almost always sealed by wisdom, for with him the
love of silence is a virtue. Melancholy and
pride breathe forth, escaping from the
depths of his soul, and diffuse themselves
over his clear and venerable face. That
man, altogether superior, detests the lie and
pomposity, avoids the full light, guards his
mental strength for his work, fortifies his
soul against adversity and follows the max-
im, 'It is better to be than to appear.' He

has never taken an ambitious step, never spoken a servile word, and there is no trace in him of that jealousy which infiltrates itself like a poison in the heart of the artist and of the man of letters; forgetting his own works, he takes pleasure in extolling those of others, and never needs to be informed by common report in order to recognize merit. I do not know a contemporary more ready than he is to hear that which is true, to exalt that which is beautiful. He carefully avoids talking, or listening to talk about himself. You must draw words from him one by one, or else divine his impressions. You would believe him soured, an egotist, a dissembler; no, no; Barye is simply a strong, loyal and chaste nature, enemy of that chattering which is the curse of our time. He talks when it pleases him, with much wit and clearness, and he could rail in a biting way, but the most discreet irony suffices him. Pushed to the wall he would be implacable and terrible, as a man who places the right always on his side. A naif and profound observer, a great sculptor, a learned naturalist, a man sensitive and not sentimental, convinced of his own worth, without vanity, solid in his

affections, despising his enemies to the point
of forgetting them, very charitable toward
others and severe toward himself, behold
him ! "

One who lived in close intimacy with
him says that, while he was silent toward
the world, alone with a comrade it was a
different thing. "He was an exhaustless
talker, a sagacious and naif critic." It is
clear, from the pictures drawn of Barye by
those who had access to the innermost cir-
cles of his friendship, that there (as for example in Rousseau's loft-studio at Barbizon
during the years of fatness), the mute and
reserved man became full of animation and
sparkle. Yet the self-restraint and the sar-
castic humor native to him did not even
then altogether abandon him.

The door admitting to his *atelier* was
closed save to his most intimate friends.
Those who entered found him working,
sometimes alone, sometimes his wife was
reading to him as he worked. M. Eugène
Guillaume says:

"The *atelier* presented a unique spectacle.
Models in clay and wax were upon the
easels, casts still unfinished upon the tables
with the tools near at hand; upon the wall

were fastened numbered drawings and models from Nature. The master, girt with his apron of worker in bronze, modeled, retouched the plaster, chiseled, inserted parts in the vice, examining them under all aspects and in every light, leaving nothing imperfect. His application was indefatigable to the very end, and only when he had done his utmost did he sign his works." Roger Ballu describes his method of building up a figure: "Barye did not plant iron wires in the base of the model . . . He modeled the parts separately, one by one, in his hands, if they were not of considerable dimensions; on a table, if they were too heavy. When he had gathered all together, he sustained the parts by exterior supports or wooden props . . . His work, as some one has said, resembled a ship in process of construction with its rigging in place." He remained thus free to the end to make whatever changes seemed wise. Charles Blanc says that on entering his house, Quai des Célestins, "you traversed a veritable museum and seemed to hear a great noise. In his studio you found a man calm, chary of speech and gesture, but of an expressive face slightly

animated by a fine smile." All agree in
emphasizing Barye's insistent vigilance,
holding his art always up to Nature. The
portfolio marked "Service," which contained his notes and numbered drawings,
the results of his observations and measure-
ments, was always within reach. In the
Beaux Arts collection of his drawings, one
can follow him through all stages, as he
models the jaguar. He studied first the
living model in the menagerie, then the
skeleton in the museum, then he took a
dead cat and, placing it in the position re-
quired, modeled it. What wonder, when
he saw a fine hare in the cook's market-
basket, he borrowed it and sometimes forgot to return it.

His contemporaries admitted his suprem-
acy as sculptor of animals. But some of
them said that he was only an animal sculptor and had no talent for representing the
human figure. Barye felt the injustice of
the criticism and remarked with some bitterness : "My brother artists, in relegating
me to the beasts, have placed themselves
below them." The two Theseus groups
and those of the Louvre pavilions furnish a
complete answer to these critics.

As Michelangelo, with whom, in the spirit of his work and life, Barye showed kinship, he was painter as well as sculptor. His contemporaries knew only his watercolors. But he worked also in oils. These canvases, however, were tightly locked in an *armoire* at Barbizon. His work as painter, by the consenting verdict of all critics, exhibits the same qualities as his work as sculptor, "grandeur of aspect and intensity of life." But Nature was for him rather a setting for his animals, whose tawny and spotted coats he admired equally with their strong and supple lines. The sentiment of Nature, as a thing to be loved in and of itself, the poetry of the earth and sky, the brush work of that grand colorist, the sun, were not his to interpret.

Charles Blanc says that his oil paintings show great vigor, character, and truth, and at a distance could be mistaken for canvases of Diaz, Décamps, Dupré, or Rousseau. The execution is not, however, as skilful. He excels only in water-colors, but he puts too much vigor into them. His skies do not agree with his earth, because he had never seen the skies of the tropics. Théophile Gautier adds, "The brush of the master acquires the firmness of the boasting-chisel. You would say that it was made of a lion's moustache."

Barye's Barbizon life is associated with his work as painter. His village home was a modest one, as modest as Rousseau's. He loved to escape thither and wander either alone about the forest or in the company of his friends Dupré, Décamps, Rousseau, Corot, Français. His great friend Millet lived there. The gorges of Franchart were a favorite hunting ground. He did not travel, and the forest must give him the skies and the settings of rocks and trees for his colored representations of animal life.

Late in July we wandered through the forest to Barbizon, by the wood paths, a walk of fifteen to twenty miles. Twice roe-bucks crossed the path a stone's throw away. One turned at our call and looked at us for the space of many breaths. A large red doe, feeding just behind the fringe of trees, waited until we had passed. Two deer in spotted coat, disturbed by a crackling branch, bounded away. In the gloaming, you will often see the wood trio—stag, doe, and fawn—feeding in a wood path, or in the strip of grass-land on the forest edge.

Wild boar are said to inhabit the wood. Rabbits and hares swarm multitudinous in the enclosed warrens and open fields until the chase opens. Occasionally a pheasant may be seen stalking across a square of ploughed land cut into the forest domain. Barye knew all the habitudes of this animal life of the forest of Fontainebleau. He saw too, in imagination, in the gorges of Franchart and Apremont the fierce life of the Indian jungles and African wilds.

Heart disease came upon the stubborn worker toward the last and held him to his chair.* Corot's death was kept a secret from him. One day his wife, dusting the bronzes, remarked, "My friend, when thou art well, thou shouldst see to it that the signature of thy works be more legible." "Be tranquil," answered the dying Spartan, "twenty years hence they will search for it with a magnifying glass."

* He died June 25th, 1875.